THE PEOPLE'S FAVORITES

SERMONS BY
DR. DALE M. YOCUM

Volume 2

ISBN 0-88019-328-X

Schmul Publishing Co., Inc.
Wesleyan Book Club   1994   Salem, Ohio

Other books by Dr. Dale Yocum:
Armies of God
Ask the Animals
Conformed to Christ
Creeds in Contrast
Dr. Yocum Teaches the Epistles of Paul, Vols. I and II
Fruit Unto Holiness
God, the Master Scientist, Vols. I and II
Hijacker in the House
The Holy Way
Job: The Perfect Man
Study Notes From My Bible,
Vols. I and II
The People's Favorites, Vol. I
This Present World
True and False Tongues

For a list of sermons by Dr. Dale Yocum
available on cassette, please contact:

Mrs. Dale Yocum
13014 West 67th Street
Shawnee, Kansas 66216

The People's Favorites

SERMONS BY
DR. DALE M. YOCUM

Volume 2

Printed by
Old Paths Tract Society, Inc.
Shoals, Indiana 47581

DEDICATION

MRS. TERRY (BECKHAM) ALDREDGE

There are relatively few students who enter college with their future occupation already very evidently "cut out" for them. Teachers and classmates in the Kansas City College and Bible School quickly recognized that with the coming of Terry Lane they had an excellent student and an unusually talented artist.

As an artist for the *Herald and Banner Press*, Terry Lane began illustrating Dr. Yocum's weekly "Bible and Science" articles in the fall of 1968.

After her marriage to Tom Beckham, she continued to produce excellent drawings for the publishing house and do covers for Yocum Books, including *Armies of God, Fruit Unto Holiness, Job—The Perfect Man, Study Notes From My Bible, Vols. I and II, and The People's Favorites, Vols. I and 2.*

Anyone who knew Dr. Dale Yocum would feel a bit of nostalgia upon seeing the cover of Volume II of *Study Notes From My Bible*. The likeness of the drawing to the man himself is much better than many photographs we've had done.

Especially outstanding among the books is *Job—The Perfect Man*. Not only is the cover excellently done, but the representation of the man under trial is graphically depicted by her art at the beginning of each chapter.

The silhouette of the author on the cover of *The People's Favorites* is, as the artist put it, "the picture of him I carry in my mind." Students he has taught and church members in his former pastorates will recognize the man at once.

To artist Mrs. Terry (Beckham) Aldredge, this book is dedicated.

Mrs. Dale Yocum

Table of Contents

SERMON 1

WE HAVE AN ADVOCATE

Holiness is to love God with all our heart,
and soul, and mind, and strength,
and to act accordingly.

My little children, these things write I unto you, that ye sin not. And if any man sin, we have an advocate with the Father, Jesus Christ the righteous: And he is the propitiation for our sins: and not for ours only, but also for the sins of the whole world. And hereby we do know that we know him, if we keep his commandments. He that saith, I know him, and keepeth not his commandments, is a liar, and the truth is not in him. But whoso keepeth his word, in him verily is the love of God perfected: hereby know we that we are in him. He that saith he abideth in him ought himself also so to walk, even as he walked.

I John 2:1-6

I am taking a phrase out of the first verse of this chapter for the basis of the message this morning: We have an advocate.

Our Father, we thank Thee for the holy, Heavenly atmosphere where Thy saints dwell together in unity. We praise Thee for

Thy Holy Spirit who has come to us, who has been our all-suffi-ciency in times of weakness, weariness, strain and perplexity. We thank Thee that through Him we can be in constant fellowship with Thee. How happy is our lot as pilgrims on this way. We praise thee Lord for the privilege of being strangers and pilgrims in the earth and for the hope that is set before us. We pray that we not only may apprehend afresh how great is our responsibility but also how great are the resources that are ours to make this journey clear to the end. Touch us afresh in this hour, and Thy name shall have our heartfelt praise. Amen.

We have an advocate. This blessed verse has in it one of the strictest charges and one of the sweetest assurances we can find anywhere in the Word of God. This is a message to little children. There are two original words for "little children" used in this chapter. One, used in verse 13, refers to half-grown children who have been weaned but are not as mature as they think they are. However, the one used in this passage means "newborn infants, darling children, darling babies." To them is given this strict charge: *These things write I unto you, that ye sin not.* But lest they despair with such a high standard, there is given this sweet assurance, *If any man sin, we have an advocate with the Father, Jesus Christ the righteous.*

I am bringing you somewhat of a Biblical tossed salad in this message—a little bit of the theological, a little of the practical, and maybe a little of the inspirational, tossed up together.

I will speak first of all about the prohibition of all sin. Second, I will speak about the provision for one who does sin. Both of these are found in the framework of this epistle, which is really a holiness epistle.

THE PROHIBITION OF ALL SIN

The fact is declared here that it is God's will, and if it is God's will it is certainly a distinct possibility, that a person live on this present earth and not sin once. In this verse, *My little children, these things write I unto you, that ye sin not,* the original indicates that not even one sin is permitted. This is a newborn child in Christ to which the writer is referring. He is not to sin, even one time. Greek scholars seem to be in agreement on this.

Now, in contrast to this verse, there is a Greek tense in other verses in this epistle which indicate repeated action instead of single, isolated events or acts. This is the case in chapter 3, where in verse 6, for example, he says *Whosoever abideth in him sinneth not.* That is, he does not go on in a repeated course of sinning. "Whosoever goes on in a repeated course of sinning hath not seen him, neither known him." Verse 8 says, "He that goes on repeating sin is of the devil; for the devil goes on sinning from the beginning." The is an indication of repeated action at this point.

The only way to interpret this epistle of St. John is in line with the doctrine of second blessing holiness. This is a holiness epistle, a very beautiful, very blessed epistle. John doesn't mention the word *holiness* anywhere in it, but this epistle is about holiness. The Bible writers were not primarily theologians; they were people who had the glorious experience of being inspired to write. John was infatuated with the love of God, so that is what he focuses on. The message is "perfect love," as it was with the message of John Wesley, but it's holiness, nevertheless. It's the same thing seen from many different human facets, different viewpoints, and different standpoints.

Let's look for a while at the meaning of this concept of sin. What is it to sin? There are two outstanding interpretations, two outstanding theological approaches, to this book, one Calvinistic and one Arminian. While the tense is different, the Greek term for *sin*, the Greek root term, is the same in these incidents—to deviate in any manner whatsoever from an absolute standard of perfect behavior. And this is the Calvinistic definition of sin. Any deviation in any degree whatsoever from an absolute standard of perfect behavior, as God sees and interprets perfect behavior, is sin. I do not accept such a definition of sin in this epistle because it is impossible to interpret or study this epistle consistently with such a doctrine of sin. With that kind of definition, this verse would read, "My little children, these things write I unto you that you not even one time deviate in any manner whatsoever from an absolute standard of perfect behavior." As anybody knows, that's an impossibility for a newborn child in Christ to walk so carefully that in no way whatsoever does he deviate from God's absolute perfect standard of behavior as He sees it and knows it. Nobody, nobody, could come up to that standard.

But the Calvinist doesn't carry that definition through, for when he comes to chapter 3 and reads, *He that committeth sin is of the devil*, using his definition, the Calvinistic would have to say, "He that goeth on deviating in any respect whatsoever from an absolute standard of perfect behavior is of the devil." The Calvinists say we have to deviate in thought, word, and deed from a standard of perfect behavior every day of our lives.

However, the Calvinist does not like this definition of sin in this context, so he changes his definition and adopts an Arminian definition of sin in this passage. For example, the *Amplified New Testament*, which has a Calvinistic bias, translates the passage in verse 6 this way, "No one who abides in him deliberately, and knowingly, habitually commits or practices sin." The Calvinist has to insert the concept of deliberately choosing to sin—the Arminian definition. The Arminian definition of sin is, "A willful transgression of a known law of God," an act involving a deliberate choice in relation to what we know to be the light of God, or the knowledge of God.

The *Preacher's Commentary*, which also has a Calvinistic bias, makes this comment about John's writing. "There are seemingly opposite truths here. Sin is wholly alien from the Christian, and the Christian is never wholly free from sin." Now isn't that interesting? Sin is wholly alien to the Christian, and yet the Christian is never wholly free from sin! That's like saying, "This man has never been in the continent of Asia, but actually he's never been out of the continent of Asia either." The writer of the commentary goes on to say that John struggled to give these two opposite truths their proper balance. That's not so. John doesn't struggle at all in this passage of scripture. It's the Calvinists who are struggling. They attribute to John what they themselves are doing, and that's judging falsely. John had no trouble because he had the right concept of sin, and they have a wrong concept of sin.

Thank God for holiness. The only way, I say, to interpret this is in the light of holiness. But I would like to go back to the Calvinistic stronghold in I John. If you've ever listened to a Calvinist over the radio very long, you've heard him get into I John 1:8. *If we say that we have no sin, we deceive ourselves, and the truth is not in us.* When I was in military service, I had a chaplain who smoked cigarettes and drank liquor. He preached about seven minutes on the average. About every third week he would try to quote this passage, although he didn't know it too well

What's John talking about here? He's talking, I say again, to little children, new converts, and he's talking to them against a background of a heresy that was prominent in that day known as Gnosticism, a certain false kind of wisdom or knowledge. The Gnostics taught that the spirit of man is good and the flesh of man is inherently evil. In other words, the Gnostics were the Calvinists of their day. They taught that sin inherently and inseparably resides in the body. Our spirits are good, but our bodies are sinful. They go on sinning, and they can't help that. The flesh is essentially depraved, and nothing in this world will deliver it. When we die, however, our spirit will go to Heaven and our old body will go back to the grave, freeing us from sin at death. That sounds like modern day Calvinism.

John was directing his remarks to this pernicious error. These Gnostics were asked the question, "What about Jesus? Did He come in the flesh? Did He have a real body?" "No," they said, "He just seemed to have a real body." They knew that Jesus was a sinless person, so to justify their position they said He didn't have a real body—He just seemed to have one. This is what John begins attacking. He said, *That which was from the beginning, which we have heard, which our hands have handled....* "We know that Jesus had a real body. We handled him. We put our hand in His side. We touched Him. We saw Him. We listened to Him. We saw Him eat. We saw Him pray. We know He had a real body." Anybody that tells us that Jesus didn't come in the flesh is of antichrist, John says. He was attacking an insidious error of that day that's carried over into modern day Calvinism.

Now, John is saying in this verse that if we go on talking like we're not responsible for this inner sin of ours, saying we really don't have the nature of sin in our body, we are liars and the truth is not in us. He wasn't battling against holiness; he was battling against the Gnosticism of his day. We as holiness people ought never to dodge around from these scriptures that are holiness scriptures. There are no Calvinistic scriptures in the Bible. They're all ours!

Now, we also have in this passage of scripture the essence of holiness portrayed ever so clearly. Holiness is to love God with all our heart, and soul, and mind, and strength, and to act accordingly. We're living in a time, however, when love is greatly perverted. We're living in a day when there is a new morality, a situational ethics, that has risen to declare that as long as you love, it doesn't matter at all what you do.

For example, Dr. Joseph Fletcher says we ought to reword the ten commandments to say: Thou shalt not covet ordinarily. Thou shalt not kill ordinarily. Thou shalt not commit adultery ordinarily. For me, he says, there are no rules, none whatsoever. Anything and everything is right or wrong, according to the situation. There is only one absolute: always to act with loving concern. Others of the same kind have actually gone so far as to describe a man visiting a brothel, a house of prostitutes, and declaring that the man came away healed in his soul. Where there is healing, there is Christ, and the angels sing "Glory to God." What sordid blasphemy!

Let me declare to you, friends, that according to the Bible, love has teeth in it! Love has principle involved in it.

Love is wedded with indignation. Love has children of zeal, passion, obedience, and carefulness.

St. John, it seems to me, sets three measuring instruments for us to use in assessing our experience of holiness: light, love and faith. In all of these measures, we have a comparison with the law.

The Measure of Light

The first one of them is light. In the seventh verse, he said, *If we walk in the light, we have fellowship one with another, and the blood of Jesus Christ his Son cleanseth us from all sin.* Light is whatever comes from God into your heart to make your duty clear to you. I praise God for the light today. I praise God that our hearts can be fixed up until we love the light. John says in his gospel, *He that doeth truth cometh to the light that his deeds may be made manifest.* There is a heart condition in a person that impels him toward the light, that inspires him to seek out the light and rejoice in the light when he finds it. The heart of a sanctified person is in a search for more light. No matter what it costs him to walk in the light, he praises God when he finds light. Some people have found fresh light in this meeting. I have. I thank God for it. I'm going to have to do some things a little different than I did before, but I rejoice in that because God is still shining His light upon me. He still loves me! I thank God for the light. The devoted child of God loves the light of God, no matter what it shows him, no matter what responsibilities, duties, sacrifices, and crosses it places in his way. He embraces it all because it's light from God. That's why we love the Word of God. That's why we love the secret place. We want the light of God shining in our heart.

But light, while it comes from the Word of God, may be a very personal thing. Love becomes extremely personal. I believe that if a person walks carefully and consistently in the light of God, God just may lead each one of us into places where nobody else in all the world understands what we're doing. I'm discovering this more and more. If we're going to walk with God, we're going to have to get to the place where even our closest friends may misunderstand us and misinterpret us, but we just know it's our light. We don't go fighting back or spouting off; we just follow the light as best we know the light.

There's a complex intersection near my home in the Kansas City area, and several roads come into it. There's a traffic light there with red, amber, and green, pointing in several directions. Under it is a sign which says, "Wait for your light." In other words, don't watch somebody else's light and go when you think it's your turn, or you'll get in trouble. I think God would give us all that motto to hang on our wall: "Wait for your light." I can't walk in all the light that someone else has, and another person can't walk in all my light, but I can walk in my light, and when I do, I have fellowship. Hallelujah! I have fellowship with God, and the blood cleanses from all sin.

Let me also say that the light of God gets very specific. In this little epistle where John talks so much about love, he really gets down to brass tacks, as we say, about some specific things. Like hating our brother. Like loving the world and the things that are in the world. Like seeing that our brother has need and shutting up our bowels of compassion against him. He says those people who do such just don't live in love. If you hate your brother, you're in the dark. If you love the world and the things of the world, you do not have the love of God in you. The light of God is in perfect accord with the commandments of God.

The Measure of Love
The second standard is the measure of love. In the second chapter, verse five, he says, *Whoso keepeth his word, in him verily is the love of God perfected: hereby know we that we are in him.* If a person consistently tries to do the will of God, it

will lead him right into perfect love. There is no other way. But in chapter five, verse three, he says, *For this is the love of God, that we keep his commandments: and his commandments are not grievous.* You start loving God, and it will lead you right into obeying the commandments of God.

You can start keeping the commandments consistently and go right into the love of God, or you can start with the love of God and it will lead you right into keeping the commandments of God. They are inseparable. They're harmonized perfectly. The end of his commandments, Paul says, is charity out of a pure heart. He says in another place that love is the fulfilling of the law.

Let me say right here that the life of holiness is not a life of legal bondage. It is not a life where we are tied and held rigidly in a straight jacket in which we constantly do a tightrope walk trying to keep up on all the minutiae, all the details, and all the commandments that have ever been uttered. It is not a legalistic, hard life. It is a life of love. *For the law of the Spirit of life in Christ Jesus hath made me free from the law of sin and death. For what the law could not do, in that it was weak through the flesh, God sending His own Son in the likeness of sinful flesh, and for sin, condemned sin in the flesh. That the righteousness of the law might be fulfilled in us, who walk not after the flesh, after the Spirit* (Rom. 8:2-4).

We have discovered in recent years a higher law that overcomes the law of gravity. We sent out a number of astronauts in their space capsules. We actually can put fire under these men and propel them out into space until they are delivered from the law of gravity. They can sit out there in their space capsules and float a pencil to one another, or just lay their Bible out in front of them and read. They are still within the gravitational field of the earth, but they are perfectly free from the gravity of the earth.

Our God has done the same thing for us in the power of the Spirit of our God. *The law of the Spirit of life in Christ Jesus hath made me free from the law of sin and death.* He has given us a lifting power. He has given us a propulsive power. He has given us a go power that has liberated us from the bondage, from the gravitation of life. He has put a lift in our soul. He has put a love in our heart, and it is not a bondage to obey the Lord. Hallelujah!

I like to be good, friends. I just get the greatest thrill of my life out of behaving myself. Praise God! There was a time when it was a hard thing to try to be good, but there's no bondage in it now! His commandments are not grievous. If the Lord suddenly breaks in and shows me something real hard that He wants me to do, I just feel like breaking down and weeping. He thinks enough of me that He talks to me about something. He'll give me grace, and I'll get a thrill out of obeying. Hallelujah!

The Measure of Faith

Another measure here is the measure of faith. John talks a good deal about faith. In the third chapter, verse twenty-three, he says something about it, *And this is his commandment, That we should believe on the name of his Son Jesus Christ, and love one another, as he gave commandment.* Here faith, love, and the law are all put in perfect harmony. Faith here is a matter of commitment and continuance. It's a matter of continuing in the light no matter what the light shows to us. The word *continuing* is used many times in scripture. This Christian life is not all a hilarious spasm at an altar of prayer; it's a matter of plodding on from day to day. It's a matter of walking a step at a time. Whatever the next step involves, I'm going to continue no matter what the hazards, what the obstacles, what the difficulties, what combinations of hellish ingenuities get in my way. I'm committed! I'm going on! This is what faith means. John says that he that believeth, that goes on believing, he that commits himself and continues, has the witness in his heart. He knows where he is. He's going on. Praise God forever!

THE PROVISION FOR SIN

Let us look for a little while at the provision for one who sins. God's love is different than what modern ethical teachers are talking about. John says here, behold, what *manner* of love the Father hath bestowed upon us. The New Testament uses a different word for this kind of love. We've been transformed by this visitation of love. It's not fleshly love. It's not erotic love. It's divine love that's been imparted to us, that's visited our hearts. These relativists talk about a lustful, self-seeking love, but this is a self-giving love, a love by which God gave Himself to us and we give ourselves to Him in return. We give ourselves to the salvation of others in return. When God sees this kind of love in our hearts, He can look over and have mercy on a lot of ignorance, a lot of stumbling, a lot of childish failures and flaws.

There was an itinerant minister who came home after he had been away for some time. He came in through the rain and his shoes were very wet. He had a little daughter who was overjoyed to see her father. She wanted to do something for her precious father, and when he slipped off his wet shoes and put on his house slippers, the little daughter found his wet shoes, put them in her mother's oven, and turned the heat up to about 350 degrees. When she thought of the shoes and opened the oven door, there was shoe smoke rolling out. When she cooled them off and brought them out they were turned up at the toe, turned up at the heel, and rolled in at the sides. What did the father do to that daughter? Did he grab her and give her a good lashing? No, he put his arm around his little daughter, kissed her, and said, "Thank you, dear, for being so thoughtful. You love your Daddy, and I appreciate it." God doesn't do any different than that. Sometimes our conduct is awkward, isn't it? Sometimes our activities give away the fact that we have a rather limited brain and a limited set of equipment that we work with, but our God looks down and says, "I see the motive." Oh, praise His name!

My little children, I write these things unto you that you just do not sin. He gives us love, He gives us light, He gives us faith, and He gives us His law to help us, so we don't have to sin. But in His grace and in the abundance of His understanding and His eternal loving kindness, He makes provision for one who does sin, for he says that *if* any man sin, we have an advocate with the Father. It's possible for Christian people to sin. It's possible for sanctified people to sin. It's not expected. It's against the rules. It must be an exception if a person is going to go on in the favor of God.

The Psalmist wondered who can understand his errors. This is an area that I think we need to explore a little bit. I think we need some practical help in identifying when we sin. Let's take first of all the area of secret or unconscious fault, the area where as far as our conscious mind is concerned, we are not declining from our love, we are not failing of any of the known responsibilities that are ours. However, as God looks down at us, He sees various places where we are falling short.

I was in the auditorium praying this morning, and suddenly I felt the Lord moving upon my heart. The Lord showed me, very sweetly, very graciously, an area of fault in my life. I don't know how much of a handicap this has been to me, or how much of a hindrance it has been to others, but I fell to weeping and praising God that He had thought enough of me to show this to me. Oh, it was so blessed how He came to me and pointed this out. I said, "Lord, I thank you. I bless your holy name for showing me that." I plan to do something about it. It was an area that had been in the realm of the unconscious. I don't know how, but God had been seeing this all the time, and He reckoned that this morning would be a good time to talk to me about it.

Do you know that the blood covered this sin, and I didn't lose fellowship with God for even one thousandth part of a second? Why, I was walking in the light! When He showed it to me, I said, "Thank God for the light!" I had fellowship and the blood cleansed. I don't know how you feel about this, but as a holiness preacher, I need the cleansing of the blood every moment that I live. There may be a hundred other things that are going on in my life that God will reveal down the way, but right now they're all covered by the blood! Hallelujah! Praise the Lord!

Here's what John Wesley said. "The best of men still need Christ in His priestly office to atone for their shortcomings, their mistakes in judgment, and practice, and their defects of various kinds. For these are all deviations from the perfect law and consequently they need an atonement. Yet that they are not properly sins may appear from the words of St. Paul, 'He that loves another hath fulfilled the law, for love is the fulfilling of the law.' " Isn't that wonderful? We thank God for the cleansing of the blood of Jesus Christ.

There may be times in our life when we are conscious that we have done something wrong, but we didn't do it deliberately. I have a very dear friend who, after he was converted, was on his cattle farm one day in his pickup truck, taking care of his cattle. He was walking in the beauty of the life of Christ. I think he had been sanctified, although he was just a very young Christian at the time. Suddenly, he let an oath slip from his tongue. It wasn't premeditated. When he realized what he had done, he went over to the fender of his truck, laid his head on the fender, and sobbed and sobbed. Here, he, who had been professing to be a follower of Jesus Christ, had uttered an oath against his Lord. He was crushed. But out of his brokenness of heart he prayed. He said that the Lord came to him in sweetness, in blessed fellowship, and assured him that their fellowship wasn't broken. The Lord had accepted his tears, his humility, and his apology, and their fellowship wasn't the slightest bit interrupted. Isn't that glorious? My, I'm so glad for the kind of God I serve. He understands us. He's interested in us. Praise His blessed name!

There was a time in my young life when I was in our country church, trying to serve the Lord. One night in a revival service, I looked across to a school friend of mine whom I admired very much. He was not saved. The Lord spoke to me, and said, "I want you to go over and speak to him." I had never spoken to anybody in a service about his or her soul. I was much smaller than he was. He was much more popular I was. I was an extremely timid soul. It seemed to me that I could lift the world on my shoulder about as easily as I could do what the Lord was asking me to do. However, I didn't rebel. I said, "Oh, God, help me now. I'm not able to do it." I held on to the seat, and it seemed to me like I would collapse in my tracks. The Lord had asked me to go. I was willing to do it. I wanted to do it if only I could summon up the strength. I could see myself staggering over there and being mute and dumb and not knowing what to say to this boy.

While I was trying to muster the courage and get a prayer through to God, the invitation closed, and I didn't go. They invited the people to come down to the altar, and I went with my head down and leaned over the altar and bawled. "Oh my God, I've failed! I've failed!" The Lord said, "I know your heart, and I forgive you. You'll do better next time." And I said, "Lord, I will, by your grace." I was keenly conscious of my fault, but it wasn't a deliberate rebellion against Him. No, I would rather have died on the spot than rebel against God. While I was trying to muster up strength in my boyhood to try to do something that seemed impossible to do, the moment passed by. I needed again the blood of Jesus Christ to cleanse so as to keep fellowship, and He did.

There is also the area of deliberate, although isolated, acts of sin, as when a person perhaps under a tremendous spiritual pressure gives way and takes that one cigarette, although he has renounced the habit. Or a person under a tremendous pressure does something else because of his weakness, maybe because he has neglected a little his devotion to the Lord. That is certainly sin. It is deliberate, but it is an isolated act of sin. Now, what about people like this? Here's the point where we need an advocate, and here's the point where John says we have an advocate. If any man sin, we have an advocate. He is dealing here still with a single isolated act of sin, the exception to the normal pattern of a Christian life.

What is the meaning of this term? An advocate is the same as a comforter, a defender, a counselor, a mediator, a patron, a legal representative who stands in our stead. In New Testament times, a paraclete was often appointed to represent a person who was penniless or a stranger or foreigner in the land. When a very poor person or a foreign person who had no ability to stand for himself went before the courts of law, a patron, a paraclete, or an advocate was appointed to go in his stead before the law and represent him. Now the judge did not deal with this man on the merit of the represented person. He dealt with this man on the basis of the advocate's merit. He dealt with the case as though it were the case of the advocate himself, a man of character, a man who had training, a man who had respectability before the court.

This is what John tells us we have in the person of the Lord Jesus Christ. We down here in our weakness, our ignorance, and our dumbness so often need to find favor with God. He says that we do not stand strictly on our own merit; we have an advocate who is interceding in our behalf before the Father, even Jesus Christ the righteous One. He's standing in my stead before the throne of God. Jesus Christ stands before the Father on His high and holy throne and says, "I'm representing Dale Yocum. He needs lots of help. He needs lots of mercy. He is so slow. He is so awkward. He's timid. He's trying to preach, Father, and I'd be pleased if you'd have mercy on him and give him favor, give him help." And sometimes I feel like He is, hallelujah! It's all because I have a representative who is pleading for me on the basis not of my ability but of His ability. He is saying, "Oh, God, help him now. He's my child. He's walking in my light. He's covered by my blood. He's following me. He loves me with all his heart. And Father I want you to give him help." And He just helps me through. Praise the Lord. We need the advocate!

We have immediate restoration. In whichever one of these categories our defect falls—whether they are totally unconscious and not deliberate, conscious and not deliberate, or conscious and deliberate, although in exception to the pattern of our life—we have immediate restoration if we walk in the light of God.

Maybe you think I've gone too far, so let me go back to John Wesley. He said, "It is remarkable that many who have fallen either from justifying or from sanctifying grace have been restored and that very frequently in an instant, to all that they had lost." M. L. Haney, another holiness man, said, "If we lose the blessing, (that is, of entire sanctification) can we be restored by a single act of faith, or must we again be first justified and then sanctified? The backslider will be restored from that state when the sins that he has committed since he was sanctified are all washed away, and that may be done by a single act of faith, precisely the same as is true of justification. If but one sin has been committed, when that one sin is forgiven, and our nature purified from its stain, we stand as before it was committed."

Sanctification and its glorious life in Jesus Christ is not a legalistic bondage of servitude, struggle, and strain. The life of holiness is not like trying to do a handstand on top of a seventy foot flagpole with a high wind blowing, even though some people approach it this way. No, that isn't the life of holiness. The life of holiness is a life of rest. How can we rest trying to live a perfect life? Because we have an advocate. Because His love fills our hearts, and His Spirit undergirds our experience. No, this isn't doing a handstand on a flagpole. This is standing squarely on the biggest rock in the universe, the rock Jesus Christ, and having His arms around us, His love within us, His Spirit undergirding us, and His hand holding our hand. Through the hardest circumstances, through the hottest battles, through the darkest clouds, He is able to save to the uttermost! Why? Because He lives, pleading for us, putting His blood down to our case, and interceding before God in our behalf. He's going to see us through! Hallelujah!

SERMON 2

FULL SALVATION

Holiness is life centered around the most glorious, captivating, charming personality in God's universe. It's to have that Person come and dwell in our house and reveal Himself to our souls and have an eternal love affair with the loveliest Person in God's universe!

I want to begin reading with Ephesians chapter three, verse fourteen:

For this cause I bow my knees unto the Father of our Lord Jesus Christ, of whom the whole family in heaven and earth is named, that he would grant you, according to the riches of his glory, to be strengthened with might by his Spirit in the inner man; that Christ may dwell in your hearts by faith; that ye, being rooted and grounded in love, may be able to comprehend with all saints what is the breadth, and length, and depth, and height; and to know the love of Christ which passeth knowledge, that ye might be filled with all the fulness of God. Now unto him that is able to do exceeding abundantly above all that we ask or think, according to the power that worketh in us, unto him be glory in the church by Christ Jesus throughout all ages, world without end. Amen.

Ephesians 3:14-21

I love mountains. I love to go to the Tacoma, Washington area and look at Mt. Rainier. Mt. Rainier is a very special mountain. It isn't just one of a whole set of mountains almost lost in the congregation of mountains; it's a mountain out all by itself: symmetrical, majestic, tall, snow-capped. From all parts of the country, for many, many miles around, you can see glorious, white-capped Mt. Rainier.

This portion of the Ephesian letter is the highest mountain peak in all the New Testament, towering up, up, and up, majestic and glorious. However, Paul assures us that this peak is for every one of us to scale, not in our own strength, but in the mighty ability that God gives us.

The Fullness of Strength

I want to look for a while at some of these provisions of God's fullness as He sets them forth in this passage. The first is the *fullness of strength* in verse sixteen. He would grant you, according to the riches of His glory, to be strengthened with might by His Spirit in the inner man. The emphasis of the New Testament is on what happens on the inside of man. Externals are important, but of supreme importance is what happens on the inside. If something miraculous doesn't happen on the inside, it doesn't really matter too much what happens on the outside.

This transformation on the inside is the Spirit's might in the inner man. A person can be mighty in spirit and puny in body. A person can totally obey God's will and be a paralytic, a consumptive, or a hobbling cripple. He can be mighty in the inner man.

The might that we need to do the will of God, to perform the work of God, is an inner might, a might by the Spirit. Paul wrote to the Philippians, *Work out your own salvation with fear and trembling, for it is God which worketh in you both to will and to do of His good pleasure* (Phil. 2:12b, 13).

I don't know what makes you unable to live fully up to God's standard, but I know it can be reduced to one of these two things: a problem in your will or a problem in your performance. Paul says that God works in you to solve the *will* problem and to solve the *do* problem. *It is God which worketh in you both to will and to do of His good pleasure.*

My dear friends, God has a fullness of strength so that you *want* to do God's will and are *enabled* to do God's will. That pleases Him. I guarantee you, on the authority of God's word, that if you are fully pleasing God, He will be fully pleasing you. Now that's great that the Holy Spirit can strengthen you so that you do what pleases God and you are pleased beyond description while doing it!

Oh, how I love thy will, O Lord. I come to do thy will. There is strength to do what is right if nobody else agrees with you. There is strength to do what is right if it's not easy to do what is right. We don't have to reduce Christianity to what's easy and what feels good when we have this might by the Spirit in the inner man. We are enabled to do what we naturally never could do or wanted to do because we have a strength imparted by the blessed Holy Spirit.

There is power to live a holy life in an unholy world. There is power to go against the current of popular opinion and popular conduct. There is power to go on doing what is right because it's right and because we'd rather do what is right than what is wrong. There is power to have clean, pure speech when all the speech around us is vile, foul, blasphemous, and suggestive. There is power to trust God when all the evidence is contrary. There is power to go on rejoicing when others are whining and complaining. Hallelujah!

My wife knows I like cookies with a bit of chocolate, and she got me a package of cookies stamped out to the same size, the same shape, and the same lines. I had forty copies of the same cookie shape to eat. Well, God doesn't stamp us all out to the image of anybody else. He calls us to different courses, different conduct and different assignments. Friends, this supernatural power of the Holy Spirit will enable you to do what He wants you to do if He doesn't want anybody else but you to do it. Glory!

It's power enough for Dale Yocum! You don't know what that means. I was timid. I was backward. I was introspective. I was born second of a set of twins, and my twin sister held that over me all the years we were together. She dated a long time before I did, and when I would complain, she would say, "Well, Dale, after all, I'm older than you are." Yes, by thirty minutes! If you knew what I came from, you could appreciate, as I appreciate, this inworking of the Holy Spirit that helps us do something we didn't think we could ever do.

I was such a midget that the first day my sister and I went to a college history class, a sweet-faced girl turned around, looked at my sister and looked at me, and said to my sister, "It was sure nice of you to bring your little brother to visit today." That didn't help my ego! I weighed seventy-five pounds when I started college! I was so homesick that first year, I wanted to go home and shoot and trap for rabbits all the rest of my life! I would almost pray for God to let a truck run over me as I walked across the street, crying, "Oh, God, I'm too miserable to live."

I still have an old aluminum recording that I made in speech class that first year in college. I had such a squeaky voice! I appreciate what God has done for me tonight! It's all to His praise. Paul said, *I can do all things through Christ which strengtheneth me* (Phil. 4:13). I think he was a runt of a fellow, too. I think he had a squeaky voice. But he said, "I can do it, if Jesus strengthens me." And so can you, friend! Whatever He's asking you to do, you can do. You have this might by the Spirit in the inner man.

I was visiting Addis Ababa, Ethiopia a few years ago, and I became acquainted with a precious girl called Azieba. She told me about her experience of going to prison for Christ. She was riding in a taxi, (this was right after Communism had taken over) and she began handing out tracts to others in the taxi. One of them was a Communist official. He said, "You can't do that!"

She said, "I can. Here, have one." He said, "We'll put you in prison." She said, "I won't stop serving Jesus even for that." So he ordered the taxi driver right up to the prison door and escorted her into the prison. He said to the prison keeper, "Keep this girl until I come back and tell you what to do with her." He never came back. She went into prison. She began to be a little fearful of what this might mean until she remembered the words of Jesus, *Fear not them which kill the body, but are not able to kill the soul; but rather fear him which is able to destroy both soul and body in hell* (Matt. 10:28).

She said, "Lord, would You please help me not to be afraid?" She reported, "All fear left, and I felt as secure in Christ as I ever had in all my life. I began to witness to this man who was personally charged with my confinement. He said, "What makes you like you are?" I said, "Because I've been filled with God's Holy Spirit." He said, "I was one time, but I lost Him. I surrendered to Communism." I said, "Well, you're the kind of person I'm sent here to talk to then." She just began to turn the heat on that Communist until finally he opened the door and said, "Would you please leave?"

I'm talking about what timid people, scared people, can become if they have this empowerment by the Spirit on the inside. Are you afraid of what God is calling you to do? You don't need God to change His mind; you just need God to change your nature. You need Him to put something inside you that will make you equal to your task, and He will. That's His pledge! Strengthened with might by His Spirit in the inner man!

This is also a fullness of Christ's own presence. *That Christ may dwell in your hearts by faith.* Paul is writing to people who already have Christ in their lives, but the emphasis here is on this word, "dwell." It's a word which, as I understand, indicates a climactic and completed operation of the Lord—something that's instantaneous, something that is completed and climactic. *That He may dwell in your heart.* He's already there, but He's a kind of guest in our house. But there comes a time when He is no longer the guest. He's the owner and operator and indweller of this house.

When we first went to Jamaica as missionaries, we stayed in the mission home with the senior missionaries there. Our terms overlapped for about three months before they were to go home for furlough. Half-way through that three month period, the two families were in devotions together one morning and the senior missionary took down the Bible as if he were going to read the morning lesson and have us together for prayer. Suddenly he did something which I did not anticipate. He handed the Bible over to me and said, "Bro. Yocum, you have been a guest in this home these weeks, but from this morning on, you're the head of this house. You're in charge. Tomorrow morning I won't draw out the Scripture and ask somebody to pray; you'll do that. From this morning on, you are the head of this house, and we are staying in your home." I had been in that home for weeks, but it was different from that point on. I was in charge.

I think that's what Paul is talking about here. Christ has been in this house. He's been dwelling here, but from this day, He's in charge totally, absolutely. He dwells here. I take the guest room, or whatever other room He wants to put me in. It's His house now; it's not my house.

My dear friends, this has to happen if you're going to know Christ like He wants you to know Him. There has to be a surrender of the whole house to His oversight, His ownership, His total control. It's not my house anymore, it belongs to Him.

This Christ is revealed within us. It would be interesting if we could hand out a sheet of paper and ask everybody to respond to the question, "What is holiness?" For many people, holiness is primarily rules of conduct: I can't do this. I must do this. I can't go here. I must go there. You do this. You don't do that. But may I say to you, friends, that such things are totally incidental to what holiness is. Holiness is life centered around the most glorious, captivating, charming personality in God's universe. Holiness is having that Person dwell in our house and revealing Himself to our souls. Holiness is having an eternal love affair with the loveliest person in God's universe! Hallelujah! I would like to lift some of our concepts of what holiness is. Holiness is delightful, it's appealing, it's overwhelming, it's transforming, it's transfixing, my friends! The dos and don'ts recede in importance when you fall in love with Jesus Christ!

Paul wrote to the Galatians and said, *But when it pleased God. . . . to reveal His Son in me.. . . .* Paul didn't talk to anybody; he went to Arabia. Scripture implies that Paul may have stayed there for three years. Arabia is not a mecca for vacationers; Arabia is a barren land. You know why Paul went to Arabia? He didn't want to be bothered while he was getting acquainted with Jesus Christ. He wanted three years just to get acquainted with Him.

Have you ever really had an inner revelation of the personality of Jesus Christ? I have! Christ has been revealed in me! I love Him tonight above everything else in the world. Do you? Does He eclipse all the things of the world? I'm troubled for the number of people who are running to the world for their excitement these days. Paul didn't look for entertainment; he went to Arabia to get to know Jesus! Oh, have you met Him, friends? Holiness is Jesus! Holiness is Jesus on the throne of your heart.

In one of my pastorates, a missionary wife came to the altar one time struggling to be holy. I tried to make holiness as simple and as beautiful as I could. Finally an insight flashed into her mind and she relaxed and started laughing and weeping. "Oh, I struggled for seven years on the mission field to do what holiness people are supposed to do. I struggled, I struggled. But oh, what rest! What a rest!" You mean this is just Jesus living His life? Yes, that's exactly what it is! Jesus living His life in me!

My mother sought holiness at a camp meeting, sometimes twice a day, for a full week before God sanctified her wholly. She really counted the cost. My father came from a holiness-fighting family, and the first night she went to the altar her husband loomed before her. The cost that she decided to pay that night was, "I'll go this way if my husband rejects me." That took a little while to settle, but she settled it. The next night she said, "I'll go this way if all my neighbors make fun of me and reject me." God sanctified her on the seventh day.

A few days later she was peeling and preparing a basketful of apples in the shade outside the house on a bench. She suddenly looked at this tedious task and said, "Lord Jesus, this is a big task, but it would be so much easier if You would just come and sit on this bench beside me and help me do the work." She moved over, and He came and sat down beside her. She wept and she laughed and praised God as she peeled apples, and they had all day together! I don't know what your task is, or what your burden, but why don't you say "Lord Jesus, come and brighten up my task. You make my day. You light up my life."

This life is a fullness of love. *That ye, being rooted and grounded in love, may be able to comprehend with all saints, what is the breadth and length and depth and height, and to know the love of Christ which passeth knowledge.* To know that which passes knowledge sounds like a paradox. How do you describe the indescribable? How can you know that which is beyond knowing? Well, you can know it in experience though you may never understand it with your mind. The love of Jesus Christ is the knowledge for which Paul is praying. It's *Christ's* love.

When I was a four-year-old boy, we had five children under school age in our family. One day we were in a little room off the kitchen, and we children were singing, "I shall know Him, I shall know Him, by the prints of the nails in His hands." As we were singing, I began to weep. My mother heard me crying and came in and said, "Dale, what's the problem?" I said, "I don't know." She said, "Are you hurting somewhere?" I said, "No."

"What are you crying about?" she asked. "I don't know," I responded. "Well, go on and sing. I like your singing." We started over, and I broke down in tears again. Mother came and said "Dale, what's your problem?" I said, "I don't know why I'm crying." She said, "Well, I think I do. You're crying because you love the One who died for you, aren't you?" I said, "Yes. Yes, that's why I'm crying."

I want you to know, friends, that from the time I was four years old and had that wonderful revelation of Christ's wonderful love for me, I have never had any desire to follow the things of this world. There's never been a day in my life, not a single day, from that day to this that I have known God's will and said, "I don't want to do it." I want to do what will please Him Who loved me enough to die for me. Do you want to do what pleases Him, or are you bent on what pleases you?

It is wonderful to know this love in an experience that can't be described. You can know it in your heart. He loves me, and I love Him. I guess that's why I become so disturbed by people who try to define holiness by rules and regulations. His love flooded my heart, and I didn't need a thousand rules. I didn't! I loved Him! I'm afraid of people who think we've got to live a holy life by tightening down the screws, and multiplying the rules. That will never do if we can't get people in love with Jesus Christ!

I'm not against rules. Rebels have to have them, and some people who aren't rebels need a few of them. I believe in rules—don't say that I want to discard the rules. But I get troubled by people who take the approach that you just push rules at people and that will help them live a life of holiness.

You say I'm exaggerating? I'm not exaggerating a bit. I have in my hand a tract written by a conservative holiness man who lists twenty rules for a holy life. In conclusion, he says, "All you have to do is start quitting the things men-

·tioned here, and any others that you know of that are contrary to God's holy Word, and you will never have to seek at another altar for the work will be done." I don't believe it! That's heresy in the name of conservative holiness. I'm alarmed by it! I really am! We've got a dangerous system when we feel we can safeguard holiness by multiplying rules. I say again that rules have their place, but they don't save anybody. You don't attract anybody to Jesus Christ by condemning every little iota of what he's doing and what he's not doing. God help us!

A president of one of our conservative holiness colleges received a letter not long ago from a man who said, "I am not supporting this kind of school any more because you talk too much about love. That's compromising." God have mercy on us. To think that we compromise by glorifying the love of Jesus Christ! God forgive us. The Pharisees could hardly do any worse than that! Belittling the love of Christ, as if it's not enough!

When we were in Seoul, Korea, we had Sunday afternoon Bible classes with some GIs. There was a Presbyterian who was invited to our Bible study who had been so addicted to beer that he drank up to forty cans a day. Then he got saved and gave up his beer. He said that as time went on he was surrounded with so much wickedness and seduction that he began to be a little fearful that he start drinking again. Reading in his Bible, he came on this word "sanctification." Fortunately, there was a friend of his in the service who knew a little about what sanctification meant and brought him to our house. He started attending our Sunday afternoon Bible studies.

He said, "What is this sanctification?" I said, "This will cross up your theology." He said, "I don't mind a bit about my theology. I want to know what this is. If it will help me to be stronger, if it's something I ought to have, then I want it!" I said, "Well, it's something you ought to have, that's for sure, and it will make you stronger." We discussed it, we wept together, we studied together, we prayed together, and I challenged him to come to God in faith.

He called me one night from the Army post and said, "It happened today! I was in a big Army truck right in one of the busiest streets of Seoul. I was praying as I was driving, and I suddenly I had a sweet pain." (I like these new testimonies. They're not trite; they're not worn out cliches.) "There was pain before I went on that trip," he continued, "but I went through my room and took down pictures that I thought maybe Jesus wouldn't like to look at. I threw away things I thought maybe He wouldn't like. I really cleaned house getting ready for this. But that pain has all turned to sweetness." That fellow, in the first week after he got filled with the Holy Spirit, witnessed to every single soul in his outfit including the Commanding Officer and the cleanup boy. My brother, this is so good!

He got ready to come back home, and he began to sense a problem with his wife who was still a good Presbyterian. He said, "I don't know anything about where to go to Church." So I made some research and pointed him to the closest conservative holiness church I could find where he was going to be stationed. He came home, his wife met him at the airport and said, "We won't be living together. I'm finished with you." She went away and married the youth pastor at their church.

He was crushed, but he held on. "I know Jesus has filled my heart. I'm going on." He was stationed near that conservative holiness church and started attending. The next letter I received from him said, "Bro. Yocum, I can't go there any longer. They're not reaching out to anybody. I can't understand this. It looks to me like we would want to reach out and tell everybody about this. I've been there week after week and they don't talk about reaching out for anybody." He left, and he never came back. That's our problem, friends.

I knew a good pastor who started a church in a University city. He was out bringing people in. God was blessing, but he had a dear sister in that church who would go down to the altar with these brand new Christians, and before they left she would get her little notebook, jot down their address and phone numbers, and the next day she'd be at their door with the rules of conduct. And they would leave and go somewhere else.

I appreciate what Bro. Beckham said last night. Do we have trust that the Holy Ghost knows how to teach a new convert? Do we really believe that the Holy Spirit is wise enough and effective enough as a teacher to take care of His own child? God only knows the harm that has been done by people who are so zealous over the little rules and regulations that they don't give the new baby time to learn to drink milk before they try to cram beefsteak and gravy into them. Again, I say I'm not against rules in their place, but when we use rules to drive people away from Christ's love, we're doing a horrible disservice to Him and to them. Oh God, help us to get some things straight in the conservative holiness movement.

Paul wrote to the Romans and in chapter twelve, that wonderful practical chapter, urged them on to holiness. *Be transformed by the renewing of your mind.* He then gives them some practical consequences of this, and one of them is that you'll be given to hospitality. The Greek word for hospitality means "A lover of strangers." I love strangers! They don't look like what we do, but I love them. Too many of our strangers feel like they're at arm's length. God help us, dear friends.

Again, I say that I'm not against rules, but I just want us to be so filled up with the love of Christ and find out what Christ wants us to do. It's not grievous to do what He wants you to do.

Oh, give us a revival of love! Make our church a hospital again. Let's bring in some broken, bleeding, soiled, dirty people and show them the love of Christ. Let's love the stranger. Let's be given to hospitality. This is the place where they can meet the Saviour, the Healer, the Deliverer. Glory be to God!

Sermon 3

Meat and the Kingdom of God

For a Christian, Scriptural principles guide our actions. We need to walk so that our life consistently reflects the love and grace of our Saviour.

Let's look into God's Word. Romans chapter 14, verses 10-21:

But why dost thou judge thy brother? or why dost thou set at nought thy brother? for we shall all stand before the judgment seat of Christ. For it is written, As I live, saith the Lord, every knee shall bow to me, and every tongue shall confess to God. So then every one of us shall give account of himself to God. Let us not therefore judge one another any more: but judge this rather, that no man put a stumbling block or an occasion to fall in his brother's way. I know, and am persuaded by the Lord Jesus, that there is nothing unclean of itself: but to him that esteemeth any thing to be unclean, to him it is unclean. But if thy brother be grieved with thy meat, now walkest thou not charitably. Destroy not him with thy meat, for whom Christ died. Let not then your good be evil spoken of: For the kingdom of God is not meat and drink; but righteousness, and peace, and joy in the Holy Ghost. For he that in these things serveth christ is acceptable to God, and approved of men. Let us therefore follow after the things which make for peace, and things wherewith one may edify another. For meat destroy not the work of God. All things indeed are pure; but it is evil for that man who eateth with offence. It is good neither to eat flesh, nor to drink wine, nor any thing whereby thy brother stumbleth, or is offended, or is made weak.

I'm speaking today about meat and the kingdom of God. You may put many other terms and considerations in this phrase instead of the word "meat," but whatever the word, I'm talking about these things in relation to the kingdom of God.

Verse 17 said that the kingdom of God is not meat or drink but righteousness, peace and joy in the Holy Ghost. Verse 20 says, "For meat destroy not the work of God."

You might be rather amazed to know how much space is given to this question of eating meat offered to idols in the New Testament. Paul gives all of First Corinthians, chapter 8, and most of First Corinthians, chapter 10, to this subject. He refers to it again in Colossians. The subject is referred to over and over in the Book of Revelations. Whether or not to eat meat offered to idols was a real problem, a burning issue, in that day.

Thank God, this issue didn't split the church. A church council was called in Jerusalem to keep this and related issues from splitting the church wide open. However, the issue didn't die at that time; it was merely held under control.

Paul treats this issue at great length. It was a complex problem. It was a serious problem. But Paul's priority was to save the work of the kingdom. *For meat, destroy not the work of God.* It's important that we don't destroy God's work in standing for truth. Amen.

We want to save the kingdom. That's what the body of Christ is. This is kingdom business that we're involved in. This was an important issue, and in treating the question of meat, Paul lays down some important principles, some important considerations.

Paul makes some very important distinctions that I want to lift up for our consideration, and I pray that God will help us understand how to approach our problems. The considerations of Paul in this passage are just as applicable to issues that are affecting us as they were to the issue of meat offered to idols.

The Distinction Between Rules and Principles

The first of these distinctions is the difference, or distinction, between rules and principles. Let me go into a bit of detail concerning this situation about meat in order to make clear what I am saying. This question came up before the council of Jerusalem: Do the gentiles have to keep all the rules that the Jews keep in order to be Christians? Now the Jews had a multitude of rules. They had 613 commandments, and a good Jew had to keep all of them. The problem was that some of the Jewish Christians were insisting that Gentile Christians had to keep all the Jewish rules.

In conference with the leaders and the local church in Jerusalem, and under the guidance of the Holy Spirit, the leadership came to a conclusion that pleased the Holy Spirit: they should not impose upon these Gentile Christians any more rules than are necessary. In other words, you don't increase grace and glorify God by multiplying regulations. There are some necessary regulations, and they named four. (It's rather remarkable that they reduced the number of rules from 613 to 4.) These necessary things were abstaining from meat offered to idols, from things strangled, from blood, and from fornication. This includes the whole range of immoral evil which was so commonly associated with idolatry.

In those four regulations, there are some things that are absolutes and some things that are relative. How many of you ever heard a passionate sermon on abstaining from eating things that have been strangled? Obviously that was a relative regulation. It was very important then, but it isn't important to us today.

How many of you have ever heard a sermon condemning fornication? That's an absolute. An absolute regulation is something that is wrong because God is right. As long as God is holy, some things are going to be wrong, forever and forever and forever. They will be issues until the end of the age because God is eternal, and He has attached His eternal, unalterable holiness to the issue. Fornication was wrong at the beginning; it's wrong today, and it always will be wrong. Absolutely. Period. It's not debatable. It's not negotiable.

There are a lot of issues like that. Issues that are made crystal clear in the word of God and attached to the unalterable holiness of God are not negotiable, friends.They are sins.There are many lists of absolute sins in the New Testament.

I recently made an extended study into the issue of jewelry. I'm more convinced than I ever have been that the holiness church's traditional stand against jewelry is exactly right, an eternal principle. I'm thoroughly convinced that the desire to wear jewelry came originally from Satan himself, and what Satan did to bring about his own fall, he always tries to get other people to do.

I see the issue of divorce in the same way. Jesus said, *Whatsoever God hath joined together, let not man put asunder.* That means that where there has been a marriage, let there not be a divorce. The Bible says that God hates putting away. Jesus said that it was so from the beginning. Moses made a few alterations because of the hardness of the people's hearts, and wherever there's divorce, there's hardness of heart somewhere. There's sin somewhere. I am equally as settled in my own mind after fairly extensive study that the adulterous marriage is sin and always will be sin. Where the Bible speaks on an issue, we have to speak on the issue.

There are many other issues. I believe this issue of women wearing men's clothing, mannish clothing, is an eternally fixed and unalterable principle in the word of God. There are many prohibitions in Deuteronomy 24, but only the wearing of men's clothing has the word abomination attached to it. When God puts the word "abomination" on something, that means the issue is eternally fixed. It's related to the character of God. This issue of women wearing clothing pertaining to men relates to the intermingling and confusion of the sexes, and the distinction of the sexes comes right out of the character of God Himself. Anything that is designed to confuse the distinction of the sexes is really a thrust at the person of God Himself. In the first chapter of of Genesis, it says that God created man in His own image: *In the image of God created He him. Male and female created He them.* Hebrew poetry states the same truth over and over again in different words, and when it says that *male and female created He them*, it's derived from the preceding statement that they were created in the image of God.

Maleness and femaleness come from the image of God. Maleness and femaleness is much more than sex. There are male qualities that come from God the Father: courage, boldness, initiation, authority, strength, and endurance. There are female qualities in the Godhead, especially from the Holy Spirit: gentleness, inwardness, and graciousness.

There are some things that are absolutes. There are some things that are relatives. This issue of meat offered to idols is relative, and Paul treats it so. In his writings under the inspiration of the Holy Spirit, Paul is saying, in effect, that if we understand the issue there might be some circumstances in which it wouldn't be wrong to eat meat offered to idols.

This is a complex issue, so let's look a little more deeply into this matter of meat offered to the idols. It is a double question: that of the meat in and of itself, and that of the associations related to the eating of this meat. This second consideration is complex. The associations have to do with who is watching us and the influence it might have on that person, and our belief concerning eating meat.

Meat was offered to an idol, and the idol didn't eat it. Consequently, the meat remained after it was offered to the idols. Sometimes the meat was burned—consumed in the flame of sacrifice—and there was no problem. There were some people who, if they should eat meat offered to idols, actually believed that a demon from the idol entered the meat. So when they ate the meat, they were taking a demon into themselves and were having fellowship with devils. Now, if a person really believed that, do you think he ought to eat it? Of course not. You had to be very careful if you believed that this meat actually had a demon in it, because if you believed that and still ate it, you in effect were saying, "Come in, devil." If you tell the Devil to come in, he'll come in, whether he comes on a piece of meat or some other way. The association was very serious.

The meat that was not consumed by the fire was frequently taken to the marketplace, and these were the choicest cuts of meat. It wasn't always labeled that it was offered to idols first.

Paul said in I Corinthians 10:20, *I would not that ye should have fellowship with devils.* In other words, if you think there is a devil in this piece of meat, friend, I don't want you to eat it. I don't want you to have fellowship with devils."

Because of this complexity of issues, the rule laid down there in Jerusalem (Acts 15) was, "Don't eat it. Period. We want to safeguard our young Christians from anything that would take them back to fellowshipping with devils." Friends, there are many situations where rules are vitally necessary to safeguard the spiritual security of the believers. We've got to have rules in our homes, and we need to have new rules when new issues arise. If we don't have rules, people do what is easiest to do, and it's easier to sin than it is to be holy in this kind of world. It's easier to drift than it is to fight the current. It's easier to just do the popular thing than to do the unpopular thing. We've got to have rules. I'm not for removing the rules but for always making love uppermost and foremost, for anointing our rule keeping with lots of divine love.

Since we've got to have some rules, they said, *It seemed good to the Holy Ghost and to us to lay upon you no greater burden than these necessary things.*

I've talked about rules, but now I want to talk about principles. That's why these three chapters are here, to help us get beyond mere rules to the principles that are involved. We don't have any problem with meat offered to idols, but the principles that Paul lays down can apply to thousands of issue that show up today and five years from now are passed away.

How do we find principles? We look for principles derived from God's holy character, His holy law, in Scripture. Whether or not to view television was not an issue at all when the Bible was written. Whether or not to wear a wedding ring was not an issue at all in the days when the New Testament was written. When we take a stand on something, we'd better be sure that we can identify a principle in Scripture that applies to this particular issue. The issue itself may not be designated in the scriptures, but there should be a principle from which this rule derives.

It helps a whole lot if we use sound reason, if we just think some things through. To move from a principle to a rule you have to think. You don't object to that, do you? Many of our issues become emotionally charged, and often we act on the basis of emotion when we should act on the basis of reason.

I've heard a couple of preachers recently say how they treat the television when they go into a motel room. One said, "The first thing that I do to that monster is pull the plug."

Another said, "When I go into a motel room and I see one of those monsters, I turn its face to the wall." If they're scared of it, if they're afraid they'll be tempted to turn it on, it's okay with me if they turn it around with its face to the wall. My wife and I carry our own radio when we travel, and the television just sits there. I'm not afraid that the Devil is going to jump out and bash me over the head. I think it would do us good to do a little thinking once in a while. Is there really something about that box that might contaminate my soul if I don't turn it around? Is the back of it more innocent than the front? Is it holier with the plug pulled out than plugged in if I don't turn it on? Does pulling the plug sanctify this demonic thing? It's easy to ride on a high tide of emotion when we're not saying anything sensible at all. When I preach, I would like to give people the idea that maybe I've been doing a little thinking about this issue.

I've been talking about this question of eating meat offered to idols, and I ask again, is there anything wrong with the piece of meat? Paul says no."We know the idol is nothing. The idol can't do one thing to a piece of meat." He's reasoning, you see.

Discovering the principles does not necessarily mean that we do away with the rules. Learning the principles may intensify our commitment to the rules. Certainly in the issue of fornication it does. When you understand that the body is the temple of the Holy Ghost, and when you commit the fornication you are sinning against the body which is God's holy temple, that intensifies our stand against fornication. We don't wait to explain all the principles to tell our children we just don't do some things. However, we should move from the rules to the principles so our people understand what the reason is for this. This is the way God treats His children.

In some cases, understanding the principles might mean that we relinquish the rule a bit. I firmly believe that if Paul had been totally in private, he could with good conscience have eaten a piece of meat offered to idols. He never tells us that. He never says, "I could do that in private," because he wants to guard his influence. He says "Do you have faith? Have it to yourself." Could you eat it? Well, just be quiet about it. Keep that to yourself. You might hurt somebody who can't by talking about it so glibly, as if it were a trifle.

There's something more than just learning a principle and from the principle deciding you don't have to keep the rules. There are associations, and those associations include our influence on younger Christians. We not only have to look at what we understand and what we can do, but at how this is going to influence somebody who hasn't learned as much as we have and doesn't understand as much as we do. We've still got to safeguard the young Christian.

The Distinction Between the Weak and the Strong

Let's go to another distinction that Paul makes, the distinction between the weak and the strong. In verse one of this chapter fourteen, *He that is weak in the faith receive ye, but not to doubtful disputations.* Here are two sets of people. One who understands the principles and can eat meat now. He understands that there is nothing wrong in the meat itself. However, here is another person who hasn't learned that. He knows the rules and he keeps the rules, and he cannot eat meat. Now, which one of these do you think is the strong one and which is the weak one? Here's one who formerly could not eat meat but now can. Here's another who is living by the rules. He never has been able to eat meat. Which do you think is the strong one, and which do you think is the weak one? You say, "Why the strong one is the one who keeps the rules. The more the better." No, that's not what Paul says. Look in verse 2: *For one believeth that he may eat all things* (including meat): *another, who is weak, eateth herbs* (never eats meat).

We're talking about a circle of faith. We are not talking about a person who has gone off the deep end in either direction: one who has cast off all rules and all principles and become a libertine, or one who has become totally legalistic. We're talking about people who are still in the faith. They still have sensitive consciences. They still want to please God. They still want to do all things to His glory. That's what Paul is talking about here. He says the one who has moved from just mere rule keeping to an understanding of principles has gained some strength in his Christian life. The one who started out keeping rules and is still at the rule level without understanding any principles is still weak in his Christian life. There is an inherent weakness about people who never grasp for an understanding of why we do what we do, who say, "We always have, and we always will. Dad didn't. Granddad didn't. I won't. Period. Don't talk to me about reasoning or understanding or principles; we keep rules here." There is an inherent weakness about that position.

The Distinction Between Despising and Judging

I want to go to another distinction, that is, the distinction between despising and judging. Verse 3: *Let not him that eateth* (that's the strong person who used to not eat meat but now he can) *despise him that eateth not; and let not him which eateth not judge him that eateth: for God hath received him.* Here are people who are doing things they didn't used to do. Don't you condemn people just because they're doing things they didn't use to do. Amen. That's Biblical, straight out of God's holy Word. And this brother over here who is still keeping the rules just like Granddad did, don't you judge and condemn this person who needs to grow and become stronger in the things of God.

I wish I had a long time to spend right here, because both of these are being done, friends. There are people who grow and understand the principles and make changes, and then they say, "Look at my brothers; they're just legalists; they're just rule keepers." There are rule keepers who see people changing and say, "They've begun to shift toward apostasy. They are compromisers." Judge not. You know what judging is? Judging is looking at external conduct and coming to an instantaneous conclusion as to what the heart has to be like. Jesus said, *Judge not according to appearance, but judge righteous judgment.* Don't you make judgments against this person until you've taken time to test his spirit. Jesus said in another place, *By their fruit ye shall know them.* Fruit is what appears which is a guarantee of the inner character.

Friends, let's be very careful about condemning somebody just because he changes. What is his spirit like? I'm still talking about the circle of believers, those who are in the faith. Let's keep peace in the family of God, is what Paul is saying. Let us follow after the things which make for peace, and things that edify another. This one should say, "How can I be a blessing to this brother?" And this one should say, "How can I be a blessing to this brother? How can we both grow up in the things of Christ together?"

The Distinction Between Liberty and Love

Let's go ahead to another distinction. That is the distinction between liberty and love. Look at I Corinthians 10:28. *If any man say unto you, This is offered in sacrifice unto idols, eat not for his sake that shewed it, and for conscience sake: for the earth is the Lord's and the fulness thereof: Conscience, I say, not thine own, but of the other: for why is my liberty judged of another man's conscience?* What's he talking about? Paul is still talking about this man who has gained knowledge, who has gained strength in faith. He recognizes that evil is not in eating the meat itself. As far as he is concerned, he can eat this meat without any kind of offence. He has achieved some liberty to eat what he didn't use to eat. "I can now do this and know that it's not hurting me. I'm not compromising with the world. I'm not compromising principles."

Listen to some things Paul says here. *We know an idol is nothing* (I Cor. 8:4). We know *there is nothing unclean of itself, but to him that esteemeth anything to be unclean, to him it is unclean* (Rom. 14:14). Isn't that liberating? We can take these things out of the context of Paul's general teaching and go off the deep end, I say, into libertineism. But I'm still talking about the circle of faith, the circle of people who put Christ first, the circle of people who have tender consciences and want to please Him above everything in the world. This is the liberty Paul is talking about, and freedom to do what I see now doesn't hurt me.

After saying this, which if taken by itself could become so dangerous, Paul immediately balanced it with the principle of love. There is more involved than just to say, "I feel free to do what I feel good about." Oh no! Wait! There's another principle that balances this, and that's the love principle. Paul really gets strict when he comes to the principle of love.

Here are some things that he says. *We then that are strong . . .* (Rom. 15:1). How do we show this strength of ours? *We then that are strong ought to bear the infirmities of the weak, and not to please ourselves.* That's a Christian principle. We're not operating by the principle that says, "Bless God, I can do anything I feel like. It doesn't matter what happens to this poor legalist over here. I've gained some freedom." People who say that have forgotten the restraints of love. These are strong principles, friends. *We then that are strong ought to bear the infirmities of the weak, and not to please ourselves.* Why? Because there's more involved that liberty. There's love.

Look at another verse, *For none of us liveth to himself, and no man dieth to himself* (Rom. 14:7). Let me read what Adam Clarke says about that: "The Greek writers used the phrase 'to himself' to signify following one's own opinion." We don't live just to follow our own opinions, just to do what we decide to do. None of us within the circle of faith is living just to do what he thinks is right. There are more important considerations than that. "Christians must act in all things according to the mind and will of God and not follow their own will." (Clarke).

Consecration settles this issue. I'm not living just to do what I feel good about. I'm not living just to do what seems to me to be all right. I'm living to represent the love of Christ, and that means that I'm considerate of this brother down here who's slow to achieve the liberty that I've achieved. He's weak, and we ought to bear the infirmities of the weak.

Look at another statement that Paul makes: But *if thy brother be grieved with thy meat, now walkest thou not charitably* (Rom. 14:15). My friends, that is one of the strongest statements Paul makes. Paul says that if the change that you have made grieves the heart of a weaker brother, you're not walking in love.

Are there people bleeding because of what you've done? If you say, "I'm going to do this anyway; I'm not living by their consciences; I'm free," then you're not walking in love.

If your brother is grieved with your meat, you're not walking charitably. There's more to be concerned with than the fact that a piece of meat doesn't have a devil in it. You need to be concerned about how your actions affect other people.

Paul states another principle here in verse 16: *Let not then your good be evil spoken of.* This passage implies that Paul himself might have eaten some of this meat if he had known that his actions would not have harmed others. However, he says here that if somebody else is going to condemn you and judge that you're not acting in a spiritual manner, then you should refrain from that action: *Let not then your good be evil spoken of.* At all times guard your reputation for Christ.

For a Christian, Scriptural principles guide our actions. We need to walk so that our life consistently reflects the love and grace of our Saviour.

VICTORY IN JESUS

I would like to take the seven sayings on the cross and dwell on them for a while. If you will follow them you can experience the victory that your heart needs, a victory that Christ has wrought for you and will work in you if you will follow Him.

I want to read from Romans chapter six. This is the most mighty doctrinal passage concerning sin and salvation that has ever been written. I delight in getting into Paul's doctrinal studies in the book of Romans. This is the very heart of what he has to say in this towering epistle of gospel truth.

What shall we say then? Shall we continue in sin, that grace may abound? God forbid. How shall we, that are dead to sin, live any longer therein? Know ye not, that so many of us as were baptized into Jesus Christ were baptized into his death? Therefore we are buried with him by baptism into death: that like as Christ was raised up from the dead by the glory of the Father, even so we also should walk in newness of life. For if we have been planted together in the likeness of his death, we shall be also in the likeness of his resurrection: Knowing this, that our old man is crucified with him, that the body of sin might be destroyed, that henceforth we should not serve sin. For he that is dead is freed from sin. Now if we be dead with Christ, we believe that we shall also live with him: knowing that Christ being raised from the dead dieth no more; death hath no more dominion over him. For in that he died, he died unto sin once: but in that he liveth, he liveth unto God. Likewise reckon ye also yourselves to be dead indeed unto sin, but alive unto God through Jesus Christ our Lord.

Romans 6:1-11

Let us pray. *Our Father, we thank You for Your Word. We thank Thee because it is the living, abiding, eternal, unchangeable Word. We're glad that through the Word of God we can have faith that is unshaken, faith that will endure anything, faith that will prevail even unto the end. We thank You for those who are crying out in their hearts for victory. We pray that thy Word may be a contribution to faith and to victory for many a hungry heart. We thank You for the way of holiness. We praise Thy holy name that through Calvary a way has been made for us to overcome sin and live in the victory of a resurrection life. Make this truth real and precious to us. Use Thy servant and speak to all of our hearts. Thy name shall have eternal praise. Amen.*

Paul writes, in magnificent terms, a great doctrinal passage about sin and salvation. In the first three chapters of Romans he establishes the universal reality, the universal responsibility, for sin. No man can come up to God with an excuse for having lived in sin. *All have sinned and come short of the glory of God.* In chapter four and the first half of chapter five, Paul writes about justification from sin, by faith, through the blood of Jesus Christ. Beginning at the middle of chapter five and going through chapter eight, he writes about the basic principle of sin, the inward nature of sin—where it came from, how it came to us, and how we have perfect victory over not only the transgressions we have committed but also over the deep stain of sin that was within us from Adam because another has come which is much greater than Adam. Thank God.

In chapter six he declares how we have deliverance from this principle of sin. In chapters seven and eight he writes about the victorious life. In chapter seven he writes that this victory is not through our own will, our own reasoning, our own morality in the law, or our own human effort. That would be total failure, a dismal, miserable defeat. But our victory is set forth in chapter eight through the Father, the Son, the Holy Ghost, and the work they do in us.

Jesus Christ not only died on the cross to do a work for us, He also died to do a work in us. Hallelujah! There is a great crowd of people today who insist that Christ's work was for us. That's it. We stand in what Christ has done for us. Paul declares that Christ died to do a mighty work in us. Paul doesn't want to leave us with any mistake about this. Everything he declares in doctrine in this chapter, he declares elsewhere in his own personal testimony. He does not teach any doctrine of which he could not testify to an experience.

We'll look at this in detail, but just take verse eleven, *..reckon ye also yourselves to be dead indeed unto sin, but alive unto God through Jesus Christ our Lord.* He gives it in personal testimony in Galatians 2:20:*I am crucified with Christ: nevertheless I live; yet not I, but Christ liveth in me: and the life which I now live in the flesh I live by the faith of the Son of God who loved me, and gave himself for me.* That's a life of victory! Hallelujah!

In verse one and verse fifteen, he asks similar questions. Verse one has to do with the state of sin. *Shall we continue in sin, [the state of sin] that grace may abound? God forbid.* In verse fifteen, he asks, *Shall we sin [there's the action of sin] because we are not under law but under grace? God forbid.* The answer is the same in both cases. We shall not continue in the acts of sin, we shall not continue in the state of sin, because grace abounds to break the power of sin and set us free.

Paul writes of this in doctrine and testifies to the experience in I Thessalonians 2:10: *Ye are witnesses, and God also, how holily and justly and unblamable we behaved ourselves among you that believe.* He didn't write a doctrinal message that he couldn't testify to in his own experience. God wants every one of us, my beloved friends, to be able to experience victory in Jesus Christ in our personal daily life exactly as Paul is writing about in this chapter. There's victory in Jesus Christ. Hallelujah!

He doesn't want us to miss the source of our victory. Four times in this passage, in verses four, five, eight, and eleven, he declares to us that our victorious life is by a personal identification with the death and the resurrection of Jesus Christ. If we can be identified with the death of Jesus Christ, we can be personally identified with the resurrection life of Jesus Christ. He died under sin once, and in that He liveth, He liveth unto God. Death hath no more dominion over Him, and sin has no more dominion over us. We can have the same kind of victory over sin that Jesus had over death. Hallelujah! That's the message of this great passage. Jesus Christ went to the cross to meet the issue of sin. He didn't just go as a martyr for a good cause. He died unto sin. He doesn't live in a continual combat with sin and death and the Devil; He lives a life totally controlled, totally given, totally lived out to the glory of God. He wants us to live exactly the same kind of life, through his victory.

Jesus Christ went to the cross as a man. He faced the issue of temptation as a man. He showed us the way to die to sin. I will never forget the thrill that came to me when I saw in the last seven sayings of Jesus Christ spoken on the cross the exact path that He has marked out for every one of us to follow if we would die the death to sin and enter into His resurrection victory.

I would like to take those seven sayings on the cross and dwell on them for a while. If you will follow them you can experience the victory that your heart needs, a victory that Christ has wrought for you and will work in you if you will follow Him.

Father, forgive them for they know not what they do.

The first saying of Christ on the cross indicated His willingness to open His heart before God and reveal the innermost content, the deepest motivation and attitude, of His heart. He said, as His first words on the cross, *Father, forgive them for they know not what they do.* If there was any person who ever had a right to have unforgiveness in his heart, any right to nourish a grudge against another, Jesus would have had such a right. He came here as a perfectly innocent, sinless person but was mistreated more horribly than any man has ever been mistreated. No man ever suffered as He did so innocently. But He opened His heart there on the cross.

He didn't say, "Father, I'm struggling with an unforgiving spirit; help me to forgive." No, thank God. He didn't say "Help me to forgive them, Lord; I have hatred for them." No, He said, "Father, you forgive them. I don't have any unforgiveness." Of course, if Jesus had had any sin in His heart He couldn't have gone to the cross as our deliverer. He went there to take upon Himself the sin of the whole world.

You and I, when we go to the cross, go there to put our sins upon Him. For Him to be worthy to take that place in our behalf, He must reveal to God that He had no sin at all. This is what He revealed. He opened his heart, exposed his innermost being before God, and there's no sin there. Thank God! He went as my champion. He went as my captain, my representative there, and He is worthy to take my place and die for my sin. He had no unforgiveness in his heart.

How different we are when we come to the cross. The unsanctified spirit so readily harbors unforgiveness. I wonder if you keep a score of the injustices that are done against you. Maybe you don't write them down in a diary. But do you have chalked up somewhere in your mind, in your memory, a record of all of the injustices that have been done against you—the people who have so falsely spoken about you, those who have cheated you, those who have done meanly toward you? Do you nourish in your heart an ambition to see them fall flat on their face and get what you think they deserve? When something good comes to them or when their face comes before your mind, does your spirit cloud up with resentment and ugly feelings about those injustices that have been done? Do you have a hope and prayer in your heart that somewhere, some day, those people will get the hurt you would like to see them get? Well, If you have that kind of condition in your heart, you need to come to the cross.

The first step is to open up before God. You can't say, like Jesus did, "There's nothing there, Father. There's no unforgiveness, there's no bitterness, there's no resentment." We have all been born in sin, and we've all had this bitterness in our hearts until we come to the cross for the remedy. The first step to victory is opening your heart and being absolutely honest. This point has been emphasized repeatedly, and we cannot overemphasize this point. There has to be a place where we're absolutely honest with God. We've quit covering things. We've quit excusing things. We've quit trying to lay them off on somebody else and paint them better than they really are. "Lord this is exactly what my heart is like. There's bitterness there. There's resentment there. There's jealousy there. There's pride there. There's vanity there. There's animosity there. There's a critical spirit there."

You say that having a pure heart is too much for any man to experience? It certainly is. That's why we're pointed to it through Christ living in us. Nobody can ever attain unto this. Paul describes in chapter seven how hard he tried to overcome that inner spirit of covetousness. He said, *I never would have known sin, except the law said, thou shalt not covet.* He got through the first nine commandments without blame, but when he came to the last one, the one which pointed to the innermost condition of his heart—*Thou shalt not covet*—he began to discover that everything he was doing was out of a covetous heart. The more he struggled against it, the more it was revealed that everything in his life was tainted by that pollution of sin. He saw the miserable uncleanness and wretchedness of his slave state to sin. Have you opened your heart before God? Have you made an honest confession: "Lord here I am, with my unforgiveness, my bitterness, and all that is there."

Stephen exhibited a pure heart at his dying. Stoned innocently by the same kind of people that crucified the Lord, he too could say as he came to die, "Lord, lay not this sin to their charge." His heart had been so transformed that he too could come down to a similar death and say in similar words,

"Lord, I have no unforgiveness. I pray for them." The witness of a man like that was so effective that Paul was convicted. When Paul came to his dying hour, he said in words almost exactly like those he heard from the lips of dying Stephen, "I pray that it shall not be laid to their charge."

Oh, the power of a life like with no unforgiveness, no bitterness! Can you take that step? Are you willing to lay it out before God and say, "Here it is?" That's the first step.

Today shalt thou be with me in paradise.

The second step is a willingness to be a witness in every area of our lives. The second saying of Jesus Christ was spoken to the thief by His side, *Today shalt thou be with me in paradise.*

There is, in fact, a two-fold witness of Christ as He came to His death. One was the witness of silence when others would have spoken. It was common in those days for thieves or criminals, as they were being put to death on the cross—their hands fastened by nails, their feet fastened by spikes—to rail and curse and spit upon those that were about them in an effort to get their vengeance upon those that had nailed them there. In the midst of that kind of a place and that kind of an atmosphere, Jesus was altogether different.

As He hung on the cross, there were no harsh words, their was no spitting at his captors, his tormentors. They prodded Him, they mocked Him, but He didn't mock in return. He didn't curse them. He didn't say one harsh or ugly word to those who put Him there. He was quiet. His silence before Pilate was an amazement to Pilate. His silence on the cross was an amazement to one of the thieves at His side. The other thief was hurling accusations: "If thou be the Son of God, come down from the cross and save yourself and us." One thief said the same in mockery, but another thief rebuked him and said, "No, we deserve to be here. This man has done nothing amiss." How did he know that? He knew it by the attitude Jesus displayed before His captors, before His tormentors. He knew it by the calmness, the quietness with which He approached this hour of death. Because of that, one thief was saved. Because of that, one of those tough Roman military leaders beheld with awe and said, *Surely this was the Son of God.*

I ask you my friend, how do you act under pressure? How do you act when people are mocking you and demeaning you and taking unfair advantage of you, turning the situation to their own good and to your hurt? What is your response? How do you act in your home under pressure?

I was in the home of a holiness pastor some years ago. I had been assigned a room where I was staying during a convention and had been there quietly for some time. The wife and some of the children came in. They didn't know that I was there in the house at the time. I heard some conversation going on. I heard the wife, who professed to be sanctified holy, scream at the son, "Shut your mouth!" I heard one of her sons scream back at her, "Don't you tell me to shut my mouth!" I don't wonder that every child in that family has gone plunging into the depths of sin. That's not holiness. No, that's not holiness.

One of the reasons why I believe in holiness so strongly today is because I saw it working in the home where I was growing up as a boy. I saw it working under trials, under poverty, under affliction, and under adversity. My mother had five little children, at one time all under school age. We lived on a farm in depression times. We had no electricity. We had no running water. We had no bathroom in our house. My mother did the washing for her farmer husband and five little children on a scrub board. She had a twisted, deformed back. She was weak in body. But with all of the work of a busy housewife on the farm, I cannot recall ever seeing my mother lose her patience, getting ugly with her children, with her husband, or with her circumstances. She lived a life under pressure. If you used all the logic you could get, you couldn't persuade me there's nothing real about holiness. I've seen it on display.

The thief saw it on display. The centurion saw it on display. Holiness was evidenced on the cross. Jesus witnessed by keeping silent. Oh God, give us that kind of a witness.

But that's not the only kind of witness Jesus gave. He not only kept quiet when others would have spoken loudly, He spoke when others would have kept quiet. He said to that thief by His side, *Today shalt thou be with me in paradise.* That's quite an announcement. He spoke the word that brought that man into paradise that day. He snatched him from the gates of hell and took him into the gates of heaven because of that witness there on the cross. In His darkest hour, He rescued a brand from the burning by his witness.

That thief exercised one of the most amazing acts of faith we find anywhere in the Word of God. I don't know that he had ever seen Jesus Christ before. We don't have the record of it, if he did. But he saw something that inspired faith. "Remember me when thou comest into thy kingdom. I recognize you as a king. I am dying by the Messiah. Lord, remember me." Jesus said, "I will remember you. Today, this very day, you're saved from hell and given access to heaven." One word of witness opened the door of heaven to a dying thief. Hallelujah! Jesus was willing to speak when others would have kept a guarded silence.

Before the high priest and the council, His accusers tried to get false witnesses. They could get nowhere with their false witnesses, and finally said, "Tell us, we adjure you, tell us the truth, are you the Son of God or not?" Jesus must speak. The honor of God was at stake. He well knew that if He said, "Yes," it would take Him directly to the cross. But it was time to speak. "Thou hast said it. I am the Son of God." He could say no less and be true to His Heavenly Father.

I said it before, and I repeat it here. God does not give us the Holy Spirit just to keep our mouths shut and be comfortable. If we don't have grace enough to speak up for Jesus Christ when others would keep a discreet silence, we don't have the grace I'm talking about. There is one thing I am praying for with all my heart, with real earnestness and fervency. *Oh God, breathe upon us the spirit of power to witness for Christ in this present age. Send us back to our churches to be a blaze of fire with boldness to witness about Jesus Christ and the wonderful Saviour of a dying world. Oh God, give us the strength, give us the boldness.* I say again, He doesn't promise to make it easy, but He promises to give us power to do what is hard.

A lady called me in the church that I pastored one time and said, "Bro. Yocum, there are some new people that have moved in close to me, and I felt that I should go and witness to them about Jesus Christ, but I'm afraid to. I just don't have the courage to do so. Do you think I need to get sanctified?" I said, "Well, it sounds like you do. If you feel so, I would agree. I'll pray for you." She prayed, called me back and said, "God has cleansed my heart. I haven't gone yet, but I'm eager to go. Pray for me that I will speak boldly, that I'll speak wisely when I speak." She did go, and God made her a blessing to that home. If you don't have the courage, if you don't have the yearning and desire to get out to the lost and share the best thing in all the world with them, then you need to take this step. If you are not willing, my friend, then you need to go to the cross and get rid of that false timidity, that false fear, that carnal fear that is holding you back from sharing the good news of Jesus Christ.

Behold thy son. Behold thy mother.

The third saying that was spoken on the cross indicates the willingness to sever every tender human tie. Jesus Christ looked down from the cross and saw His own dear mother. He saw John the beloved near by. He said to His mother, *Behold thy son.* To John, He said, *Behold thy mother.* We believe that Joseph was dead by this time. Mary was left a widow, and Jesus was the eldest son. By all the rules and practice of those days, the eldest son should have responsibility for the care of his mother. That was Jesus' responsibility. But He had said to others that he who loveth father or mother more than me is not worthy of me. Now He has to put it in practice in His own life. Is He willing to give up His own mother, willing to break those tender ties that bound Him to the most lovely soul in all the world? He could do no less and be true to the will of God. So He let that tender human tie be snapped asunder. He must do the will of God.

Let me tell you, friends, that when it comes to this matter of absolute surrender to God, God doesn't just play around the margins of our life. He will reach right in and touch the dearest things to your heart. When He deals with Abraham about faith and obedience, He doesn't reach for Hagar or Ishmael or even Sarah. He reaches for Isaac, the dearest person in all Abraham's life. Let's not equivocate about this. God doesn't fool around with secondary issues. He's going to have first place, central place, or He won't have any place at all. If He's reaching into your life, He's going to put his finger on the thing that means the most to you in all the world, whether it's a wife, a child, a sweetheart, a business relationship, or an ambition. *He that forsaketh not all that he has cannot be my disciple.* This is rugged. It was rugged for Him to look down on his own precious widowed mother. Widows had a hard lot of it in those days, but He had to do the will of God.

I served on a mission field a number of years. One of the most outstanding examples of sacrificial missionary life I've ever known was a married lady with two boys. She lived comfortably in a little bungalow. When she found this beautiful way of holiness, she began to follow God in the way He had marked out for her. The Lord surprised her one day by asking, "Are you willing to be a missionary?" She said, "Lord, I couldn't understand such a thing. I have the responsibility of two children." Her husband had already left her at this time, and she had two little boys to support. She said, "Lord, what do you mean? How could I possibly go to the mission field. I'm not even trained. How could I?" The Lord said, "I'm not asking you to explain how, I'm asking you whether or not you are willing. After prayer and after counting what might be the cost, she said, "Lord, I'm willing. I don't see the way, but if You want me to be a missionary, I will."

She sold the house. She took the two little boys along to Bible school and began to prepare herself for missionary service. It wasn't long until one of those little boys became sick and died. Before she finished her training, the other was old enough to join the army, and before long he was killed. She was left all alone. She went to the mission field, and while she was there she heard of the death of her separated husband. She was very much alone. But I have never seen a person pour out her life in more self-giving sacrifice to save others. She had made a consecration to God.

Are you willing for that kind of severing of the ties that would draw you to earthly attachments, earthly comforts, and earthly relationships? Are you willing to say, "Lord, I'll do anything, I'll go anywhere." My, what an outpouring of lives and service there would be if everybody here would absolutely sever the ties of business, comfort, home conveniences, and material gain and say absolutely, "Lord, I've let every tie be broken. I'm free from all attachments. I will follow Thee wherever You send me."

My God, my God, why hast thou forsaken me?

The fourth saying of Jesus indicates His willingness to die the death to sin. After these words that He spoke to His mother, darkness descended over the face of the earth, and for about three hours there was the most awesome darkness that ever settled on the face of the earth. During those three hours Jesus said nothing. Silence prevailed—an awesome, fearful silence and darkness. Jesus went into that darkness. After that darkness had passed away, He speaks once more in those agonizing indescribable words, *My God, my God, why hast thou forsaken me?* He had gone into the depths of the darkness of hell and sin and death. I agree with a German writer who says that during those three hours he believes that Jesus, in his spirit, was tasting the reality of separation from God, the reality of hell, the reality of the end product of sin. He was feeling what it is for a man to be under the dominion of sin to its ultimate end—separation from God. He suffered that darkness too deep for words. He tasted the darkness of hell.

This is what sin brings every man to unless he's delivered from its bondage. Unless we recognize this awful dark nature of sin, we'll never cry out with all of our hearts for deliverance. Oh, that God would give some souls a revelation of what sin really is. Sin is enmity against God. Sin is separation from God. Sin is darkness where God wants there to be light. God wants us to be radiant with the light of the glorious gospel of Jesus Christ, the God who commanded the light to shine out of darkness and shine in our hearts to give the light of the knowledge of the glory of God in the face of Jesus Christ. What a treasure to have the light of God in the face of Jesus Christ right here in our hearts! What a treasure to have heaven within our souls!

A person with that kind of experience ought to have some brightness, some radiance, some joy, some praise, some uplifting hope about his life. There ought to be a lilt in his laughter. There ought to be a leap in his heel. There ought to be a lift in his faith. There ought to be a luster about his life. Christ has come to live within his soul! But how many people there are who have a dismal, dark, depressing, discouraging darkness in their souls. That's the principle of darkness. That's the cause of separation that's leading to eternal loss— that dark, self-seeking, self-preserving, self-exalting principle in the heart that draws back from giving God full sway in the life. The principle of darkness is not willing to cast everything into God's hands and say, "He is faithful. He will do what He has promised." This is the darkness of unbelief.

Oh, the horror of this sin in the heart that does not dare to believe the almighty God! The Word of God brought the heavens into existence, and after the heavens are rolled up as a scroll, the Word of God will go on forever. That dark sinful heart says we don't dare to believe a God like this. It desires to keep going on in its own strength, its own struggling.

My friend, unless you see the darkness, the horror of sin, unless you abominate it, loathe it, desire to be free of it so you can glorify God and praise Him with all your heart, you'll never find victory. Jesus saw the darkness of it. He faced up to it. He endured it. He didn't back up. He went through it so you don't have to go through it. But you'll go into darkness forever unless this sin is taken out of your heart and you are purified in the blood of Jesus Christ. Because the end of sin is separation from God. There is separation here and separation hereafter unless God radically removes sin from your heart which keeps self in first place.

Don't be surprised if, in your seeking after holiness, you come to a place where it looks awfully dark. This principle of sin produces darkness. When you come face to face with what it really is, it'll look dark to you. Don't get frightened. Jesus made a way through the darkness. He went into it, but He came out of it. He made a way through it so we don't have to stay in this darkness forever! Glory be to God!

I thirst.

The fifth saying of Jesus on the cross was a cry of thirst. He said, *I thirst.* Of course He thirsted. He had been without food or water for many, many hours. He had been without sleep. He had lost blood. This produced thirst. He had refused to take the sponge with its vinegar. He didn't want to deaden His senses to what He was going through. He was thirsty for water, but there was a deeper thirst than that. In Psalm 69:21 we have a prophecy of this very hour, which speaks to us about the vinegar and the gall that was given to Him there on the cross:*They gave me also gall for my meat; and in my thirst they gave me vinegar to drink.* In the third verse of this Psalm, we find that there is another kind of thirst that was involved. *I am weary of my crying: my throat is dried: mine eyes fail while I wait for my God.* He was thirsty for God. He had just said, *My God, my God, why hast thou forsaken me?* Why am I left alone? Jesus said, *Blessed are they that do hunger and thirst after righteousness, for they shall be filled.* Are you thirsty? Is there something in your heart that says, "Take the world, but give me Jesus? All it's joys are but a name. Let everything else go, but give me Jesus."

I remember how thirsty I was as a high school boy. I loved to play basketball, but I came to a place when I wanted something else far, far more than I wanted basketball. Oh, how I wanted God to come and cleanse out of my heart the envy, the quarrelsome spirit, the jealousy that was there. I walked home from high school time after time praying. I would be so overwhelmed with the hunger of my soul that I would just quit walking and climb up among the bushes at the roadside to pray. "I want You to purify my heart. I want to know You face to face. I want You to fill my whole being. I want to be under Your control." I remember times when I would go out to the field to plow corn and I would just let the horses go on, put the reins aside and lift up my heart to God. "Oh, God, I'm so tired of my selfishness, my quarrelsomeness. Please come and purge my heart." I was thirsting after God.

I remember going through the barnyard gate one day, driving up the cows, and I just let them go. I was crying out to God. I took a little stubby pencil out of my pocket and I wrote on the gate post as I went through the barnyard gate, "Oh God, I will be Thine, and Thine alone forever." I meant it! I still mean it today. I want God more than anything else in all the world. He said if you get thirsty, if you really get thirsty, if you want God more than you want a boy friend, if you want God more than you want a comfortable home, if you want God more than all else that the world could heap at your feet, you'll find Him! Ye shall be filled!

It is finished.

The sixth saying of Jesus indicates a conclusion of His personal struggle. He said, *It is finished.* We are told that He shouted this word with a loud voice. This is contrary to the normal death of a man on the cross. It was customary as people's lives ebbed away on the cross that the muscles of their chests became gradually paralyzed until their breath became shorter and shorter. Finally they were not able to breathe at all. They died by the paralysis of their muscles. Jesus straightened Himself, took a deep breath, and shouted at the top of His voice, *It is finished.* What a triumphant word! They haven't taken His life from Him. He has lots of life left. *It is finished!* What is He saying? He's not saying "I'm already dead." He isn't saying that the price has fully been paid. He's saying, "My part is done now." Hallelujah! "I've run the journey. I've finished the course. I have obeyed My Father. There's not one more thing for me to do but die. My part is finished."

I'm so glad He didn't stop short in the garden of Gethsemane. I praise God that when He began to face up to the horror of this hour, when He saw the cup that He must drink, when He sweat as it were great drops of blood, He didn't turn around and flee. He set his face toward the cross. I'm so glad that in Pilate's judgment hall when the crowd was mocking Him and saying, "Crucify him," He didn't say, "Father, You must let me off here. I can't take that." He went straight on. I'm so glad that when they bared His back, bent Him over the frame, and began to lash Him with the scourge until His back was bleeding and raw, He didn't say, "God, I can't take any more." He didn't get up and run. He went straight on. I'm so glad that when they put the cross on His back and drove Him like a beast up the hill of Golgotha until He fell under the weight of it, He didn't say, "I've had enough. I give fellows, I give." No, He went straight on. I'm so glad that when He saw this horrible darkness and shrank under it, He didn't quit. He went right on.

He went the whole journey. He made the whole trip. Now He has the right to say, "It is finished. The journey is done. I've done everything you asked me to do, Father. I'm willing to give up my mother. I'm willing to give up my friends. I'm willing to make the journey." God had touched Him at every point that hurt in His life, and He went straight on.

I'm glad to tell you, dear friends who are seeking after this experience of grace, that you can get to the place where you know—as well as you know anything in all the world—that your part is done. You can get to the place where if you lived a thousand more years you know that God could not touch another area of your life that isn't surrendered to Him. God has been obeyed. You've given up everything and you know it. Glory be to God! "My part is finished. There's nothing left for You to touch. You know it and I know it Lord. My part is finished."

I go to people at an altar sometimes and say, "Have you surrendered everything to God?" "Well, as far as I know," they often reply. That's not far enough. You can get to the place where you can say, "Yes, I know I have. I've surrendered everything I know about and everything I don't know about. It's all given up to God. Absolutely." Hallelujah forever!

Well this isn't the victory of sanctification yet, but it's a place to shout anyway! Jesus shouted when He got to this point, and we have a right to shout when we get to this point, even though we're not sanctified yet. It's a mighty good place to be when you know everything is yielded to God, because victory is just beyond this.

Father, into thy hands I commend my spirit.
The last words of Jesus were those words of simple trust in the faithfulness of God. *Father, into thy hands I commend my spirit.* "Lord God, You know my part is done now. Everything else is up to You, Father. I know You're faithful. I know You will take me through this ordeal. I put myself now into Your hands." He gave His life away with those words. You say, "How do I die to sin?" Just exactly like He died to sin. The world didn't take His life from Him. The cross didn't take His life from Him. He just put His life into God's hands. When He knew that His part was finished, He knew God would be faithful in doing His part, and He simply rested Himself on the faithfulness of God. "Father, I put My life now into your hands." That moment He died.

When you get to the place where you can say, "My part is finished. I know it is. God knows it is," there is only one more simple act—"Lord, I just lay my whole life over into Your hands." There it is. That's how you die. "God, I know You're faithful and all the rest of the responsibility is Yours. I've now done my part." Jesus isn't struggling now. Men don't struggle when they're ready to die; they struggle to keep from dying.

Of course the devil comes in and whispers at a time like this, "You don't dare. He'll abandon you. He'll leave you in the grave." Jesus said, "Father, that's Your responsibility. My part is already finished. I don't have to worry about graveclothes. I don't have to worry about rolling stones away. All the rest is Yours, Father and I place Myself into Your hands now." Isn't that glorious? Oh, hallelujah! Praise the Lord! God is faithful. That's our basis for everything. Jesus rested Himself on the faithfulness of His Father. He had obeyed His Father. He had come here at the command of His Father. He believed His Father. He placed Himself in the hands of the Father. He died. Did God forget Him?

For three days it looked like it. For three days death reigned. Satan danced a jubilee. The earth waited. But God hadn't forgotten His dear Son. On the morning of the third day, the earth quaked, the rocks rent, graves burst asunder, the veil was rent in twain, graveclothes fell off, and the stone was rolled away. Christ came forth in resurrection life, in victory over sin, in victory over death, in victory over hell, in victory for all eternity. That's the victory He wants to share with us. That's the victory He bought for us when He went to Calvary. If we follow in His steps, we can enter into that kind of life of victory. Glory be to God!

If your heart is hungry, you can have this kind of victory—a resurrection victory that lifts us up out of our sin, out of our fear, out of our unbelief, out of our bondage, out of our defeat, out of our failures, and into His resurrection victory. Hallelujah!

SERMON 5

SPIRITUAL HYPOTHERMIA

Draw the line. Get your standards from the Word of
God. Get your feet on the solid rock, Christ Jesus,
and stand for something.

I'm reading today from Matthew 24, beginning with
verse seven.

*For nation shall rise against nation, and kingdom against
kingdom: and there shall be famines, and pestilences, and
earthquakes, in divers places. All these are the beginning of
sorrows. Then shall they deliver you up to be afflicted, and
shall kill you: and ye shall be hated of all nations for my
name's sake. And then shall many be offended, and shall
betray one another, and shall hate one another. And many
false prophets shall rise, and shall deceive many. And
because iniquity shall abound, the love of many shall wax
cold. But he that shall endure unto the end, the same shall
be saved. And this gospel of the kingdom shall be preached
in all nations; and then shall the end come.*

Matthew 24:7-14

These verses give a rundown of the events prior to
the second coming of the Lord Jesus Christ. I share the belief

of many that the beginning of sorrows, as spoken of in verse seven and following, came right on the heels of World War I "when nation shall rise against nation, and kingdom against kingdom." I'm not going to defend that position today, but I join with those who believe that we are in this time of sorrow, a renting, dislocating travail, as that which precedes a birth. If that be true, then these succeeding words describe the times in which you and I are living. My text here is from verses twelve and thirteen: *Because iniquity shall abound, the love of many shall wax cold. But he that shall endure unto the end, the same shall be saved.* Just before Christmas in 1963, a Greek luxury liner caught fire in the Atlantic. All the passengers on board were forced into the water. They floated on rafts or on bits of wreckage for a few hours until a rescue ship came by. Nevertheless, 124 passengers died, and 113 of them died, not by drowning, but by a condition known as hypothermia—getting too cold in the water. The water temperature was not horribly cold—sixty-five degrees, but they died after being in that water for several hours. This was proved by autopsies on many of them. I am speaking today on spiritual hypothermia—what happens to people spiritually when the temperature around them keeps dropping.

In this message we will look at this scripture from a number of standpoints: first, the result of cold; second, our responses to the cold; and third, our recovery from the cold.

The Result of Being in a Cold Environment

What is the result of being in a cold environment? Physically, the result of a hot body being in a cold environment is for the temperature of the hot body to drop. That will unavoidably happen unless there is a source of heat energy that will help it to withstand this loss. I repeat: when there is a hot body in a cold environment, there is always a drain away from the hot body to the cold environment unless it has a source of energy to replenish the heat supply and help it to overcome the drain.

This happens to people spiritually. A hot cup of coffee left for a while becomes a cooled off cup of coffee. A white hot saint in a cold environment will become a cooled off saint unless that saint maintains contact with a constant source of replenishment to keep his or her temperature up. We are living in a cold environment today. I certainly don't have to prove that point. Jesus said that because iniquity shall abound, the love of many shall wax (gradually become) cold.

The original language here reads, "The love of the many," which means "the majority." Apparently Jesus is saying that conditions are going to become so bad, iniquity proliferating on every hand, until the majority of people are going to cool off in that atmosphere. If you are going by the majority opinion, you're going in the wrong direction. If you're getting your index from what most people are doing, you've got the wrong indicator. If you are measuring yourself by what most people are thinking and doing, you're measuring yourself by the wrong standard. If you're adjusting to what the majority feels today, you're cooling off. It isn't safe to follow what the majority is doing. However, this practice is exceedingly popular. As a matter of fact, to get your moral standards from what the majority believes is standard operating procedure in our culture.

Some time ago, the public schools in our area issued a statement on their moral philosophy to this effect: "We decide what is right or wrong for our students on the basis of what the majority in our community holds to as being proper." Anybody who does that is holding a wrong standard. They are going in the wrong direction. They're heading for a wrong destiny. But that's the popular way in our culture. I tell you this, when it's popular in our culture, when our churches are not standing against the culture, the churches will adopt the standard of the culture and will follow it right on down.

The following statement was written by a professor of law at Boston College and published in *Current History* some time ago: "Obviously, a general breakdown of standards is under way. Family ties are more readily broken. Churches have lost their controlling effect on the behavior of their members. Middle class values no longer appeal to the youth, and the display of corruption enacted by the adult world on all levels attest to the confusion of end and practice." The church has lost its controlling influence on the lives of its members. That's not all. If people have gone to the world instead of going to the church, it's partly because the church has gone to the world.

I heard of a pastor in one of our so-called holiness Bible colleges stand up and ridicule the standards of the church in which he was saved. He belittled their practical standards of separation from the world and said before that assembled student body, "Before I would go that way (he was talking about old-fashioned standards as we call them), I'll go to hell." About all I can say to that is, "Amen." If that's his choice, that's probably what will happen.

That same man is widely publicized. I saw an announcement of a great crusade near the east coast some time ago at which he was one of the featured speakers on "How to win them to the church." One of his methods was outlined: "When the public high school is having a football game, clear away a great space in the church, bring in a rock band, and entice the people leaving the football game to come into the church and enjoy rock music for a while." That's not bringing the world up to the standards; that's bringing the standards down to the world. That's not applying the fire of God's truth to the world; that's applying the world's cold to our standard and to our spiritual life.

Responses to a Cold Environment

I want you to consider with me for a while how a hot body responds when placed in a cold environment. Specifically, what happens to people when the temperature around them continues to drop? What are the signs, the medical symptoms, of hypothermia? I'm going to give you these medical symptoms because they have a spiritual counterpart.

The first symptom to appear in a human body when the temperature drops around it is the shivering reflex. A person, while shivering, generates as much heat in his own body as a person sawing wood by hand. That's a built in response, a protest against the dropping of the temperature. That response is designed to generate muscular activity in order to raise the temperature on the inside to withstand the dropping temperature on the outside.

Lot "shivered" when he first went to Sodom. He was vexed. He was astounded by what he saw around them. His righteous soul was indignant because of the conditions of the cold sinful world around him. There was a protest. But shivering is costly business. Shivering consumes enormous amounts of energy, and you can't shiver forever. When the temperature has dropped as much as four-and-a-half degrees, the body stops shivering. The protest lasts for a little while, but if the temperature drops a little bit more, the tendency is to stop shivering. The spiritual tendency is to protest for a little while, but if it's obvious that the temperature is going down anyway, the tendency is to stop protesting. That's exactly what Lot did.

I'm talking about waxing cold, a gradual, progressive, downward tendency. A spiritual person will rise up and protest the cold, but if he is not extremely careful, he will soon stop protesting just because the temperature has gone so much lower.

We had an example of that when President Carter arose indignantly and opposed the Soviet build-up in Cuba. The build-up continued, so he came before the media again and said that he guessed it wasn't so bad after all and maybe we shouldn't protest any more.

This happens in the spiritual world. People see something wrong and raise a protest. The world will back off a little, and we'll feel that the infraction is just too small to protest. For example, a person puts on a thin wedding ring. It's such a sweet symbol of a love affair. Is that really worth protesting? If you don't protest that, it will be followed by the diamond engagement ring. After all they're cheaper to buy in a pair. Both are very symbolic, and both are very precious. If we allow that to pass, then there will come a class ring, or a business ring. After all, it really does stand for something meaningful. Then there will be a lodge ring. Then a big diamond ring . Where do you protest with such small degrees? Is it really worth a protest? Well, there has to be a line drawn somewhere. If we lose our protest, we're in danger of losing our life.

Friends, I don't like to hobby on anything. I don't believe I'm a hobbyist, but the Lord has brought me back again and again to some practical issues. If we don't draw a line and protest on some things, we won't protest any where. If you don't even shiver, you'll die. If you don't draw a line some where, you won't draw it any where, and if you don't draw it any where, you'll die of spiritual hypothermia.

I mentioned some outward symptoms, but really, friends, the fundamental problem is not in externals. The fundamental problem, as Jesus said, is in the love of our hearts. We can't see that. It's a lot easier to point our finger at rings and hairstyles and dress. But the root problem, Jesus said, is what's happening to the fire burning in our heart, what's happening in our love for Jesus in response to His love for us. It's so easy to cool off and stop shivering. It's so difficult to stage an effective protest against the dropping temperature around us that the tendency is to quit shivering, quit protesting.

The second symptom is a state of weariness, of weakness, of apathy. I'm not talking now about something exceedingly painful. I'm talking about the pain being over. We have so spent ourselves that a sense of apathy, a sense of weariness, has set in. "It's going to happen anyhow. There's really not much use of praying about it, or opposing it, or even standing up against it any more." It's difficult to keep our love white hot, friends, when the church world as well as the secular world has adopted this cooled off, complacent pattern of fainting. It takes a lot of energy to keep your temperature hot. It takes a constant intake from Heaven to withstand the dropping of the temperature.

With as much grace as I know how, and with as much kindness as I know how, let me say that this tendency to become cool in our love affects older people just as much, if not more, than it does our young people. We are inclined to heap our displeasure on the young people, but it's a lot easier to stir up a young person to white hot love for Jesus than it is an older person. Young people have a future to look forward to, and they are attracted by the bid for money, or marriage, or fame, or popularity. Older people are pretty well past that; many of their desires died physically a long time ago.

I'm getting older myself and I'm not here to heap criticism and blame on older people. I am saying, dear friends, that this is an area which besets everyone of us. You say you have run your course, you have fought your battle. Well you haven't fought your last battle until you cross the river. One of the most subtle battles we have is to keep from just settling down. If we're not very careful, friends, we can take on a position of criticism and fault-finding of others and not recognize that our own love is departed.

Jesus spoke to the church at Ephesus, a church that was fighting furiously to maintain the standard, bringing people to trial and condemning them for compromising. Jesus said, "You people in Ephesus are getting rather old now, getting up in years. You have lost your first love." Is it fair for me to say that we ought to watch very carefully the tendency to become excited about standards and neglect maintaining the fire in our own heart? Jesus said that we must pray always and not faint.

The third symptom of hypothermia is the clouding of the consciousness until a person doesn't think straight. The brain becomes inefficient when the temperature drops about six or eight degrees. A person out camping may have a tent in a pack on his back and may have a food supply in the pack, and yet become so disoriented in his mind that he doesn't even remember that he has food to eat. As the temperature drops, he dies with available help as close as the back pack.

One document describes it this way. "Judgment will become impaired, a fact that may imperil the safety of others in the party. A leader cannot be depended on to lead his people in the right direction when this stage arrives, because he's lost his own sense of orientation. The brain loses its proper sense of direction, and the leader may lead his party in this direction thinking it's the right way, when the other way is the right way." This is what happens physically.

Precisely the same thing happens spiritually. There are people leading willing followers, and because they are renowned leaders, they are depended on to take us to Heaven when they're not even going toward Heaven. They've lost their sense of direction. They're totally disoriented. This is an extremely serious situation when people—instead of searching the Word and asking God to reveal the truth to them—conclude that because a person is in a position of leadership he must be safe to follow. If he is not following the way to God, he is not safe to follow.

Over thirty years ago, I went into a seminary to do some research and came upon a thesis on file there. The student who had written this thesis had done some research in the area of traditional, Biblical standards of separation from the world. He had consulted with the leaders of his group, and this was the conclusion that he wrote into his thesis: "The leaders of our group have decided, in connection with the standard of separation, that they have two issues to consider: whether we shall maintain our traditional standard of separation from the world, or whether we will abandon them in the hope that we will get bigger faster. The leaders of our group have made the decision that we will abandon the traditional standard of separation from the world in order to grow faster."

You don't have to wait very long after making that decision before people begin going that way. The decision was made, not because of a deeper study into the Word, but because it would make the movement more popular.

This is a stage of hypothermia when people are disoriented and befuddled in their spiritual lives, not knowing the difference between the way to Heaven and the way to Hell. Today, in that same group, there is no battle whatsoever in these standards that we've talked so much about in our meeting here. That battle was lost over thirty years ago.

The real issue today is in the authority of God's word. A group that one time stood solidly for the inerrancy of the whole Bible is now discussing the issue of whether the Bible is really inerrant or not. Leaders in the group are abandoning the old position. They say that they never did stand for inerrancy, but that's false, and it's been proven false. That's the issue of today.

I ask you, friend, what are we going to do when the leaders, in so many areas, are heading in the wrong direction with a lost consciousness of where they are and where they're going? We have to draw some lines and stand somewhere. We will be accused of being fanatics wherever we draw the line, but if we don't draw some lines and hold them, we're lost.

A fourth symptom of hypothermia is a state of hallucination, combativeness, and a resistance to help. A person will fight against people who try to get him out of his hallucinations and back into reality. He becomes belligerent.

There are people who at one time stood firmly where I stand today who are being antagonistic against me. I am standing where they once stood, but I have become an enemy to them. I suspect there are people right here today who are being criticized by the very ones who brought you in to a conservative holiness standard. They brought you into it, but now they're denouncing it and trying to get you to change because they have changed.

I think of a young lady, a very precious lady, who I have heard testify with such power upon her that others fell under deep conviction and ran to the altar while she testified. She was a beautiful example of Christlikeness, of modest womanhood, of holiness character. Her spiritual hypothermia didn't happen all of once; it happened by subtle degrees. There was shivering, but the shivering stopped. The shift went on and on. The last time I saw her I could hardly recognize her as the same person. Whenever anybody else follows in the way which she has gone and joins the same church she has joined, she says it gives her such a good feeling.

Another one who joined the same local church as she did testified to some of his friends, "I'm so free now. I'm not bothered by those old restrictions. I can do anything I want to."

The fifth symptom is apparent death. There comes a time when the heart stops beating, when the temperature drops to the low to mid-eighties. That doesn't mean he's really dead, however, because many people have been resuscitated out of hypothermia. In fact it is easier to resuscitate a person whose heart stops at eighty degrees than it is to resuscitate one whose heart stops at ninety eight and six-tenths degrees. According to some of the medical authorities, no one is dead until he is warm and dead. You can't be sure if this person is totally dead or not until you get him warmed up. He may not be beyond recovery just because there are no signs of life. One must bring revival to him. It may be that his heart will beat again. That's good news, and I'll say some more about that.

The Remedy for a Cold Environment

I want to speak finally about the remedy for the cold. Hypothermia brings one of the most comfortable deaths there is. A person dying from hypothermia never knows when he is dying or when he's getting real close to death. I'm here to say it to all of us, friends, that if we follow this cooled-off route, don't protest it, just back off and let down a little, it is a sure way to spiritual death. You can die spiritually as certainly this way as if you stood with doubled fist and blasphemed almighty God.

Jesus said that he that endureth (and the word endure means to stand your ground) to the end, the same shall be saved. Thank God for people who will resist.

Remember, I'm talking about the majority going down and the minority standing in their place. It's popular to move today. It's popular to change. It's popular to drift. It's popular to compromise. Let me tell you, those people who decide to just accept the status quo will find out that there is no status quo. There is no stopping place. A person who says he will just settle down to ninety-three degrees will find the temperature will go down beyond ninety-three degrees. The world is so cold around us that there is no stopping place in the process. If we can't see to stand, if we can't see to protest, brother, there's no stopping place.

I'm not asking for ugly belligerence. I'm asking for a sweet protest. We're going to be sweet about it when we draw the line, and we won't cross this line, so help us God. You may not draw the line in exactly the same point that I do unless we're getting it out of the Word of God. But there are some places we need to draw the line when the Bible doesn't tell us specifically where to draw the line. The Holy Spirit has to tell me, and the Holy Spirit has to tell you.

I'm appealing to our precious young people today. Be people who stand for something. Draw the line. Get your standards from the Word of God. Get your feet on the solid rock, Christ Jesus, and stand for something. Sure, there'll be an invitation to go where it's easier, where it's more popular, where you don't have restrictions, but, if you don't have any restrictions at all, you're just going to cool off and die. That's all there is to it. Let us stand for Jesus.

Second, let us resist sleep. Jesus said in the Olivet discourse that the last age is a sleepy age. While the bridegroom tarried, they all slumbered and slept. The sense of drowsiness becomes so oppressive. It's far easier to go to sleep and die in your sleep than it is to stay awake and resist the cold.

If everybody else is getting a television, it's easier to get it and go along than it is to hold out against it. The more there are who get it, the more pressure comes on those who don't have it. There's nobody who will ridicule you more on the television issue than the people who used to stand against it but now have it. People out in the rank cold world won't condemn you over rejecting television like people who one time rejected it and have now decided to go along with it. They've become combative. They'll ridicule you.

Peter, speaking also of the last days, said there will be those who will seduce you through the lust of the flesh. They will promise you liberty, but they themselves are brought into bondage. If you let them bring you into bondage, your last end is going to be worse than your first. Resist the sleep.

There was a young lady in Ohio who was diagnosed by medical specialists as having suicidal tendencies. He recommended that she be put in a hospital where she could be constantly under security and observation. The family wanted her in their home, but the doctors said that someone needed to monitor her all the time lest she slip out and commit suicide.

For many days they maintained this watch around the clock with their daughter. One night it was the mother's turn to sit by her daughter's bedside. She had had a particularly busy day and hadn't taken the nap she should have had. She finally lay down by her daughter, put an arm across her, and tried to fight sleep. But in such a comfortable position she soon fell asleep, and when she roused her daughter was gone. She had gone to the river, jumped in, and taken her own life. It's a drowsy age in which we are living. You and I friend, have to keep fervent in our spirit.

Jesus spoke to the church at Laodicea and told them that except they repent He was going to take their candlestick out of its place. "Be zealous and repent." He said. Zeal refers to hotness in our spirit, the warmth of our devotion.

The third remedy is to warm the person who is in danger of dying. Don't isolate them. Don't cast them out. Get something warm around them. Get something warm into them. Share your love with them. These are days when we need to stand close together, when we need to share with one another, encourage one another, and warm the hearts of one another. This is no time to be ripping one another asunder and casting one another out.

A school bus in Colorado became stranded in a horrible blizzard. No rescuers could come to them for several days. The driver ran the motor as long as he could until the gasoline supply ran out. He had a whole bunch of children in there with the temperature dropping. There was not enough clothing to keep them warm. The bus driver knew that if he let them go to sleep they would freeze to death. He took his coat off and put it over the one who needed it the worse. He kept going up and down the aisle slapping and cuffing and stirring these children while they cried, "No! Leave us alone!" But he kept moving them, and finally the rescuers came and the children were saved.

We have to warm one another. We have to challenge one another. Peter said, talking of the last days, "Above all things, brethren, above everything else, have fervent (hot) love one for another." Divine love is the answer. Divine love is the fire. Divine love is the warming of our hearts. Let's keep our love alive. Peter then says, "This kind of love covers a multitude of sin." What does he mean by that? This kind of love does not expose the defects and faults and sins of others of our circle. It doesn't parade it, it doesn't publicize it, This kind of love puts a covering of love and healing over it and tries to get it all straightened out with the least publicity possible.

Above everything else, love one another. Cause your brother to stand up. If you're standing up, help somebody else to stand. Jesus tells us what the majority was going to do. The majority was just going to let it happen. But He also talks about those who endure, who stand their ground and determine that they are not going to let it happen. One of these days Jesus is going to come back.

Let me point out one verse in this chapter before I go ahead. Jesus talks about His servants in these days of long waiting. He said, "The servant who watches and maintains readiness will receive rewards from his lord when he comes. But if that servant begins to say in his heart, 'My lord delayeth his coming,' and shall begin to smite his fellow servants, and to eat and drink with the drunken, the lord will cast him out [cut him off] and appoint him his portion with the hypocrite." It's terrible to go out and eat and drink with the drunken. But as far as I can see from this scripture, it's just as wicked to smite your fellow servant. This man does two things because it just seems like he's waited so long. He begins to smite his fellow servants, and he begins to eat and drink with the drunken. Either one demonstrates that he is not really ready for his master to come. Jesus said, "Watch, and be ready, for his coming."

My encouraging word is that there's enough love for us if we'll keep in touch with it. There's a fire burning if you'll keep it in your heart. God has love to help everyone of us to overcome, to resist graciously, but strongly; sweetly but firmly. He has enough love to keep us until He comes.

A general was captured in Bataan during World War II and was imprisoned in Manchuria. While the war dragged on, he was kept in this prison, much of the time in solitary confinement. His captors scorned him, demeaned him, insulted him, and misinformed him, trying to brainwash him into total capitulation. They told him that America had lost the war. They told him he would never get out of this prison; he might just as well abandon his Americanism. But the general resisted. He didn't get newspapers. He didn't have a radio. He didn't get a ray of truth from the outside, but he had character on the inside. He was loyal to his country. While they insulted him, lied to him, demeaned him, and starved him into an emaciated heap of skin and bones, he still remained American and true in his heart.

After years had gone by, a message was slipped in to him from an American colonel telling him that America was just about to win the war. The general was jubilant. It had been worth it to hold out. Some new guards came in and started the usual process of demeaning him and giving orders, but this emaciated fellow stood to his feet, tall and frail, and said, "No! I am in command here! I am an American general. I am not defeated, you are defeated. I am the victor here." He was! He withstood the process until victory came. You and I can withstand until victory comes!

Make a firm resolve in your heart. "I will endure the cold. I will fight back. I will maintain my resistance."

SERMON 6

THE PRAYER OF JABEZ

A Prayer for Revival

We need a revival of intensity when there comes back a groan, a passion, a throb, an "Oh" in our praying and our praising. Jabez had this in his prayer.

Let's bow our heads and look to the Lord in prayer. Father, we thank Thee tonight for your presence. Thank You for the privilege again of being here in Your service, with Your people. We're sure there are needs that must be met. There are heart desires that You have the ability to satisfy. We pray that You would breathe upon us afresh tonight. We know that we're inadequate in ourselves. All of our sufficiency is from above! We look into Your open hand tonight for blessing, for grace, for a fresh touch upon our hearts. Help us, and we shall give Thee all the praise and the honor and the glory. In Jesus' name. Amen.

Turn in your Bibles to I Chronicles chapter 4, verses 5-10:

And Asher the father of Tekoa had two wives, Helah and Naarah. And Naarah bare him Ahuzam, and Hepher, and Temeni, and Haahashtari. These were the sons of Naarah. And the sons of Helah were Zereth, and Jezoar, and Ethnan.

And Coz begat Anub, and Zobebah, and the families of Aharhel the son of Harum. And Jabez was more hon-

ourable than his brethren: and his mother called his name Jabez, saying, 'Because I bare him with sorrow.' And Jabez called on the God of Israel, saying, 'Oh, that thou wouldest bless me indeed, and enlarge my coast, and that thine hand might be with me, and that thou wouldest keep me from evil, that it may not grieve me! And God granted him that which he requested.

I want to speak about the prayer of Jabez. Jabez stands out in this long list of strange-sounding names. He's a note of brightness, of hopefulness. He prays a prayer for revival, a prayer that I wish all of us could pray, because when Jabez prayed this prayer God granted him that which he requested.

When someone gets his prayers answered, I think we have something to learn from them. I'm still trying to learn how to get my prayers through—some of them get through, and some seem as if they don't. But here was a man who got his prayer through. His prayer is not known for its length; it's not known for the eloquence of the prayer. It's known for the fact that God heard him and God answered him. I wish all of us could have a prayer life that God respected so much that He would just give us everything we asked for.

The Character of Jabez' Prayer

The first notable aspect of his prayer was that it was a **prayer of passion.** It begins with a two-letter word "oh." That speaks of intensity. Some reality is just too awesome, too wonderful, too impressive to press into words, and for those rich and intense realities we use exclamations: "Oh!" "Ah!" "Wow!" These exclamations go beyond what we can put into words.

That's the kind of praying the Holy Spirit does. When the Spirit is interceding He does so with groanings that can't be pressed into English words.

Jabez prayed intensely. I looked in the index of an old Methodist hymnal for songs that began with the word "Oh," and there were 240 lines that began with that exclamation. The hymnists were trying to express something that they couldn't put neatly into words. If we are in touch with God at all, we're in touch with this reality that cannot possibly be put into words.

I counted a thousand "Ohs" in the Bible (according to my *Young's Concordance*). Here's one of them from the prayer of Isaiah: "OH, that thou wouldst rend the heavens, that thou wouldst come down, that the mountains might flow down at thy presence, As when the melting fire burneth, the fire causeth the waters to boil." Oh, that God might come down and cause the mountains of indifference and prejudice, of rebellion, of hardness to melt and flow as volcanoes flow.

Does your heart cry out for that tonight? Is there an Oh!!! in your cry? "Oh, Lord, rend the heavens! Come down in our midst! Cause things to melt in Your presence!"

There's an "Oh" in the praying of Jeremiah, chapter 9: "Oh, that mine head were waters, and mine eyes a fountain of tears, that I might weep day and night for the slain of the daughters of my people!" This Oh represents the passion of grief and sorrow over apostasy, departure from the living God.

God honors intensity. God is fire, and fire is always intense. Scripture never suggests that the lukewarm praying of a half-hearted Christian avails much. But the fervent prayer of a righteous man availeth much!

When the revival of the Hebrides really broke forth in a mighty demonstration of God's power, a teenage boy by the name of Donald was praying in an assembly. With a passion he was claiming God's promise, *I will pour water on him that is thirsty.* Donald said, "Lord God, I don't about anybody else but here's one person that's thirsty. And You made a promise that You would pour water on those that are thirsty." God rent the heavens and came down in the Hebrides.

Is there a teenage youngster here that has a passion after God tonight? Is there a young man or a young lady who has an "Oh", a throb in his or her prayer, in his or her hunger after God? If there is, God's listening! If there is, God's interested!

God abominates a lack of spiritual intensity! The church at Laodicea is a good example. This church thought they had everything they needed. They were perfectly satisfied with themselves! But the Lord said, "I am sick of you! You don't know what I think of you! You think you're rich and have everything you need, and I say, "You're miserable and wretched and poor and blind and naked. I'd rather you be cold than lukewarm." Lord, help us!

We need a revival of intensity when there comes back a groan, a passion, a throb, an "Oh" in our praying and our praising. Jabez had this in his prayer.

J. H. Jowett said, "The ill of all ills is the lack of desire." When people get to the place that they are just perfectly satisfied as they are, they don't have any passion after more. That's the sorest ill there could be to a professing Christian.

William Law said—listen carefully, "If there are no yearnings, sighings, no deep movings of soul, strong searchings of heart, is it not a mistake to call ourselves 'children of God?' "

Down in our part of the country many years ago there was a man driving a team of horses with an old fashioned buggy. Apparently the horses were frightened and started running when they hit something and tore that buggy all to pieces! Neighbors came in and found the driver of the horses sitting in the midst of the wreckage, sitting on the ground and staring blankly into space.

They hurried and asked him if he were hurt. He didn't answer; he just sat staring into space like an owl. He didn't frown. He didn't cry. He didn't respond. He was as impassive as a stone.

When they sized up the situation they started laughing. It was rather humorous, but he didn't laugh. Apparently he had bumped his head and was totally out of touch.

I think there are a lot of people like that today. Our world is in a wreckage of moral principle, a wreckage of homes, a wreckage of church solidarity. There's a great many people sitting in the midst of it all with their hands folded, with a kind of a "ho-hum" attitude.

These are times that demand an "OH!" in our souls, a passion in our praying. Revival comes when we have a burning, yearning desire after God. He doesn't come in response to a half-hearted concern.

Jabez' prayer was a **prayer for progress**: *That thou wouldst enlarge my coasts!* We believe that Jabez lived in the days of the judges. And in the days of the judges, the people were beginning a process of surrounding little pockets of the enemy and letting them remain. This process of adaptation and concession and then compromise was a deadly thing in the making.

Apparently Jabez realized this. He had a prophetic insight into where this kind of casual concession could lead his people. He was praying here for an enlarging process to continue until Israel had acquired all that God wanted them to acquire—a passion to keep moving forward. That's so vital!

Jabez is a young man we never would have known if not for this passion of his soul. "Lord, keep us moving. Don't let us ever just settle down and accept what we have. Lord, put a spirit of forward movement in our hearts!"

Please turn to Chapter 2 of I Chronicles, the last verse. I believe that this verse talks about Jabez. It says, "And the families of the scribes which dwelt at Jabez; the Tirathites, the Shimeathites, and Suchathites." Some commentators believe that this place was named after the same Jabez that was offering this prayer. Families of scribes dwelt there, and some commentators believe (and I hope they're correct) that this man Jabez established a college. The town became known as Jabez. There were three types of teachers called scribes: the Tirathites, professors of song; the Shimeathites, teachers of prayer; and the Suchathites, teachers of prophecy who taught people to proclaim God's truth.

Jabez didn't just offer a half-hearted prayer; he was earnest in an effort to change the situation. He was just one young man—his brothers weren't interested. We don't know anything about his father, and his mother was melancholy enough to call her baby boy "Sad Sack" (that's what Jabez means). But little Sad Sack decided that one boy could change the whole picture if he got in touch with God, and he established Jabez College and got a professor of song, a professor of prayer, and a professor of proclamation. Why, that's apostolic! That's what happens in every real revival! There's a renewal of singing, a renewal of praying and a renewal of proclamation when people really believe in the Lord Jesus Christ.

If we can sing, pray, and proclaim with the anointing of the Holy Ghost, there's no telling what God will do, Friends! We don't proclaim well until we pray well! And I'm tempted to say we don't pray well until we sing well—at least let's think about that order. We need the Spirit for all of these activities.

The situation that confronts us today is not vastly different from the situation that confronted Jabez. We're in a time when there are all kinds of concessions being made to the world. We allow little pockets of compromise, little pockets of sinfulness, little pockets of carnality to remain untouched and uneradicated. This is a deadly process by which we concede a little here and a little there, and we stop moving forward as God wants us to move forward. Jabez' prayer is a prayer for progress! "Oh, Lord enlarge our coasts. Help us to reach areas that we haven't reached yet. Help us never to settle for the status quo. Lord, don't let us adopt the idea that we have to just hold what we have." Wouldn't it be sad if we adopted the outlook that if we move in any direction, it's bound to be compromise, and thus conclude that we must stay exactly where we are and hold exactly what we've got and do things exactly like we've been doing them, not going forward at all.

Well, here was one young man that wouldn't settle for that. He said, "Lord, help us to go forward." Amen! Let's move forward! I believe it's still possible today if we can get young people with a passion that Jabez had.

In the third place this prayer was a **prayer for provision**. *That thine hand might be with me . . .* (v. 10). That's a lovely, rich figure of speech: "God's hand with us," and it's used over and over in the Word. "The hand of the Lord was with them." I don't know all that Jabez might have had in mind when he prayed that prayer, but let me suggest a few things that it might mean where we find God's hand.

For one, it means "fresh vision." Ezekiel, the prophet, said, "The hand of the Lord was on me. And he carried me out in the spirit of the Lord and set me down in the midst of a valley which was full of bones." When God's hand is upon you, you don't really know what's going to happen. You don't know what God's going to show you; you don't know for sure what He's going to do with you because God's hand doesn't conform to anybody else's hands. If God's hand is upon you, get ready, Friend, something is going to happen, something fresh and wonderful.

I wish every one of us would pray, "Lord, put your hand on me during this next week and let me know what you want me to do." Are you ready for that? God's direction may not be traditional, it may not be what everybody else is doing.

When God put His hand on Ezekiel, He said, "Go and preach to dry bones." Now, that doesn't mean that everybody has to go preach to dry bones, but let's ask God to put His hand on us. "Lord, what do you want me to do? Go and pray with a neighbor? Ask an enemy to come out to dinner? Take my car over and bring some orphans to meeting?" I don't know. Just ask God to tell you.

In one of our churches in Kansas City a truck driver got converted. At one of the very next services, he brought 42 people with him. God's hand was on him!

The hand of the Lord is a hand of deliverance. After the Israelites passed the Red Sea, they sang this song of victory, "Thy right hand, Oh, Lord, hath dashed in pieces the enemy." God's hands stand for a mighty, supernatural supply of power and authority, moving obstacles, overcoming enemies, and breaking bands of bondage. God's hand is a hand of deliverance still.

I was in Springfield, Illinois a few weeks ago and became acquainted with a young man by the name of Richard Yelton. He'd been on drugs from the time he was nine years old until he was twenty.

I asked him why he had this craze for drugs. "Well," he said, "when you commit crime every day to get your drug supply you get tired of yourself. And one of the biggest motivations to take drugs is so you become desensitized to the villain, the scoundrel that you really are."

"Then, of course," he said, "the appetite itself keeps mounting up. I've gone up the whole scale from the tamest to the wildest of drugs. I hated myself. I hated society. My wife left me and took my little boy. I had one friend, but he was in prison.

"I decided to pay his bail, so I robbed my own wife of five hundred dollars, paid my friend's bail, and brought him to my apartment and showed him some kindness.

"When I took a shower that night, my friend stole everything in my apartment but the clothes I had in the shower room. I was at the bottom. If I'd still had the gun I would have shot myself. I got a telephone directory and looked up some church that might help me. I called a Catholic priest and said, 'I'm going to commit suicide if I don't get help.' The Catholic priest said, 'Call the suicide hotline' and hung up the telephone. I said, 'He doesn't care!' And I came to another number and it was the phone of Bro. Wilson Douglas." One of the prayer partners answered the phone, and Richard Yelton said, "I'm at the bottom. I'm gonna commit suicide." And the lady said, "No, don't do that. We have a prayer chain and we'll start praying for you, Richard. Why don't you come to prayer meeting tonight?" And he said, "I will."

They told him how to get there, and he hung up and he said, "What did I say that for? I'm finished with the church." He'd seen some hypocrisy among Christians and written them off as frauds, but he went to the prayer meeting anyway.

When he got to the prayer meeting at the little church, people reached out their hands to him. They smiled at him and showed him love and concern. He said to himself, "This is different." When Bro. Douglas finished giving a little Bible lesson, he invited any needy person to the altar. Richard was on his feet, starting to the altar when he said to himself, 'What am I doing this for? I don't go to altars. There must be a God dealing with me."

He prayed through that night. A week later I was there in a service and his wife and son came to the meeting. They sat together.

I'm talking about a God who answers prayer and who can deliver the sorriest cases when He gets His hands on people. OH, lets pray that the mighty hand of God would be on some people!

Again, this hand is a hand of chastening. In one of David's penitential Psalms, he said, "Day and night Thy hand was heavy on me." God's hand was heavy because of unconfessed sins. David's bones were getting old and his spirit was becoming dried out. God's hand weighed him down so heavily that he finally made his confession, got straightened out and went on singing his way to victory.

I wouldn't be surprised if there are some people right here that God already has His hand on and He's going to keep pressing you down until you get real honest and make an honest and thorough confession. Praise God, He has an answer!!

God's hand is a hand of guidance. The Psalmist, praying again, said, "If I take the wings of the morning and dwell in the uttermost part of the sea, even there shall thy hand lead me and thy right hand shall hold me."

David was running from God, but wherever he went God's hand was still on him, drawing him back. Praise God, He's able to follow the runaway. He is able to follow the one who is in rebellion, the one who is in flight. God's hand will follow you there! And He can bring you back to a place of surrender, a place of victory!

You may have heard the story of Monica, the mother of Augustine. She was so afraid that her son was going to the world and going to wickedness that she prayed with passion that God would save him and not let him go to Milan, Italy. But he went.

She poured out her burden of heart to one of the saints of God and that dear saint of God said, "God could not possibly deny a prayer like you're praying." And sure enough, Augustine, in Milan, came under the ministry of Ambrose, that early church father, and he himself was soundly converted. God didn't answer her prayer just like she asked it, but He gave her the desire of her heart in the conversion of her son.

The hand of God can go anywhere a person is running and guide them to a place of victory.

Wherever you are, dear Friend in trouble, God knows how to lead you into perfect victory—from right where you are! You may not know the way, but He knows. Thank God for a mighty hand that can guide us through to real victory.

Finally, this prayer of Jabez was a **prayer for purity**. *That thou wouldst keep me from evil, that it might not grieve me.*

I've already said there was a tendency in Israel at this time to make concessions and compromises and bypass pockets of enemy resistance. There were whole towns that were left behind, unsurrendered to God's people. These towns grew and grew, finally becoming deadly enemies to God's people.

Jabez saw this, and he prayed, "Lord, let me never become adjusted to the growing commonness of evil. Don't let me ever accept little concessions and little compromises that grow and multiply and adulterate and defile and weaken and destroy. Lord keep me sensitive to every little spot that could grow and produce my downfall in the days to come."

Jabez wanted a sensitivity to sin. Like the hymn says:

I want a principle within of jealous, godly fear.
A sensibility to sin, a pain to feel it near.
Help me, the first approach to feel of pride or wrong
     desire.
To check the wandering of my will and quench the
     kindling fire.

That's the prayer of Jabez.

Samson was one of those who by little concessions and little compromises lost God.

One time when I was pastoring, a lady who had been a holiness missionary on a mission field came to our home and said, "Bro. Yocum, I don't know where I am today. I know I'm lost from God, but I don't know how to get back." Her darkness began with tiny little concessions. "Other people were compromising, and they seemed to be spiritual and have good victory. I decided to follow suit. Oh, it hurt my conscience a little bit, but not a whole lot, you know. I didn't think it was a very important matter. But now I'm a long way from God, and I don't know how to get back."

My wife and I counseled her, prayed with her. I don't know where she is today, but her downfall began with little concessions, little adjustments.

In the first night of this revival effort, I felt we ought to open the altar to anyone who is honest enough to admit, "I have lost the keenness, the freshness, the brightness of God's presence in my heart." What better time to restore your relationship with God than on the first night of a revival. What better time than now to recover the brightness, the newness of God's glorious presence in our lives.

THE NARROWNESS OF JESUS

I'm interested in knowing how narrow Jesus is. If He is narrow, then I want to be narrow. Let's look at the narrowness of His teaching and ask ourselves how narrow we should be in our teaching.

I want to speak to you this morning about the narrowness of Jesus. My text is from the last chapter of Jesus' Sermon on the Mount, Matthew 7:13-14:

Enter ye in at the strait gate: for wide is the gate, and broad is the way, that leadeth to destruction, and many there be which go in thereat: because strait is the gate, and narrow is the way, which leadeth unto life, and few there be that find it.

Let us pray. *Father, we thank Thee for being with us here today. Thank You for this camp meeting, the sense of Thy presence that is increasing among us. How we praise Thee for this. We love Thy presence, Lord. We want Thy manifest presence among us. Oh, may it increase until every soul here will be overwhelmed with a sense of Thy presence and Thy glory among us. Guide us now in our consideration of Thy Word that we may be true to Thy Word and true to Thee. In Jesus' name. Amen.*

We are in a time when many people are trying to broaden Jesus until He fits in every community and every society. There's a great effort among the homosexual community to fit Jesus among them. They tell us that the Bible does not speak about Jesus' love for women, saying He spent His time alone with men. "He fits right in with us, you know."

There's a great desire to make Jesus fit among the rebels and the revolutionaries. Pictures show him with long hair, and rebels say that He was always attacking the establishment. "He's one of us, you know." There are so-called Christian Communists, Christian Revolutionaries, even Christian Atheists today—people who believe in Jesus but don't believe in God.

I'm interested in knowing how narrow Jesus is. If He is narrow, then I want to be narrow. Let's look at the narrowness of His teaching and ask ourselves how narrow we should be in our teaching.

There are some people who don't like the restrictions of the Sermon on the Mount, so they become dispensational in their application and say that these teachings do not apply to us today. They're reserved for the millennium. That is not true. The Sermon on the Mount is Jesus' charter of the kingdom of Heaven, the heart of the teaching of the kingdom of God. When He began His teaching, He said, *Repent, for the kingdom of Heaven is at hand.* It is not reserved for the millennium. It's here now. He said furthermore, *The kingdom of Heaven is within you.* It is not reserved for the millennium. It is here and now, and it begins in our hearts.

There are three areas that I would like to identify in Jesus' teachings in the Sermon on the Mount (and elsewhere) where He consistently was most strict in His teaching.

The Motive of the Heart Examined

The first is His emphasis on the motive of the heart. We are told that at the beginning of this Sermon on the Mount a great crowd followed Him, and He spoke to them.

Among them probably were some scribes and Pharisees—at least Jesus makes frequent reference here and throughout His ministry to the scribes and Pharisees. He says in Matthew five, verse twenty, which many call the key passage of the whole sermon, . . . *except your righteousness shall exceed the righteousness of the scribes and Pharisees, ye shall in no case enter into the kingdom of heaven.* Now that teaching wouldn't fit into our modern citywide campaign. The modern citywide campaign would seek out the leading Pharisee and give him a seat on the platform. "Here's your seat, friend. Do you have anything to say to this audience? Would you like to endorse this campaign?" Jesus wasn't appealing for the endorsement of the scribes and Pharisees.

The scribes and the Pharisees were an exceedingly strict people, but the motives of their hearts were not right. Jesus was interested in the hearts of these people. He wasn't rude to the Pharisees. Luke tells us of three times in which Jesus was invited into the home of a Pharisee, and He went to eat with them, to teach them, to show them the way of truth. Probably the greatest, the most beloved, words Jesus ever spoke were spoken to a Pharisee, Nicodemus. *Nicodemus, ye must be born again.* John 3:16 was spoken to a Pharisee, *For God so loved the world, that He gave His only begotten son, that whosoever believeth in Him should not perish, but have everlasting life.* Probably that Pharisee became a believer of Jesus.

Certainly the greatest Christian since Jesus was a Pharisee before he met the Lord, and Paul became so enamored by that vision that nothing else could equal his love for the Lord. Jesus loved the Pharisees, but He told them the truth. He wouldn't compromise because He loved them too much to compromise the truth with them. Jesus interpreted the law in terms of the heart. Repeatedly in this Sermon on the Mount He repeats statements of the law or the Pharisees' interpretation of the law, and says, *Ye have heard of old times, thou shalt not commit adultery, thou shalt not kill, thou shalt love thy neighbor and hate thine enemy, but I say unto you.* . . . In every case He goes to the heart. "You have heard by the law, thou shalt not kill, but I say unto you, if you hate, you're a murderer already. If you look on a woman to lust, you are an adulterer already. Love your enemy. Do good to them that despitefully use you, bless them that curse you. Pray for them. For God loves the good and the bad and sends His rain upon both. You should be perfect, as your heavenly Father is perfect."

The very heart of the religion of Jesus Christ is in the heart of men. Paul summed it up in that song of love, First Corinthians, thirteen: *Though I have all gifts, all prophecy, all knowledge, though I give my body to be burned, and don't have this kind of love, I am nothing, nothing, nothing.* The scribes and the Pharisees were exceedingly strict, but they did not have God's love in their hearts.

It was one of the scribes who came to Jesus and said, "Master, what is the first commandment in the law?" Jesus said, *Thou shalt love the Lord thy God, thou shalt love thy neighbor as thyself. On these two commandments hang all the law and the prophets.* Everything else revolves around them. You have to have love in your heart. Now that doesn't mean that if we love God, we can go and do as we please. For Jesus made it perfectly clear, that if we love God, we will keep His commandments.

I want to read three statements to you from John chapter fourteen. *He that hath my commandments and keepeth them, he it is that loveth me* (v. 21). "If a man love me, he will keep my words (v. 23). *He that loveth me not, keepeth not my sayings* (v. 24). If you don't have a fervent desire to keep God's commandments and please Him, you don't love Him. John puts it like this, *This is the love of God, that we keep His commandments and His commandments are not grievous.* There's no grief in doing anything that God wants us to do if we love Him. The love of God means that we just want to do everything He wants us to do. We want to please Him supremely.

It is possible today, as it was then, to so focus on the external details of religious performance that we allow love to leak out of our lives. The Ephesians did. They were maintaining a very strict external religious lifestyle. They were holding to the line, bringing false apostles to trial and finding them liars, but they had lost their first love. Jesus is very, very narrow at this point. It doesn't matter how strict you are outwardly if you have lost the love out of your life.

Hypocrisy Condemned

There was no sin that Jesus more soundly condemned than the sin of hypocrisy. Throughout His teaching, including four times in the Sermon on the Mount, He speaks against this issue of hypocrisy. In chapter twenty-three of Matthew, He speaks about it eight times. Oh, how utterly devastating He was in stripping away hypocrisy and getting to the heart of things.

There are several things that Jesus classified as hypocrisy, and I want to mention a couple. One of them was the substitution of outer form for inner reality. Three times in the Sermon on the Mount, He takes up the type of religious exercise of the scribes and Pharisees—the fasting, the praying, the giving of alms—and said, "Don't do like these hypocrites do. They are doing it for the impression they have on the people around them instead of a means of prevailing with God and being what God wants them to be." Their outward life was just to be seen of men, and not to please the heart of God.

Who were these Pharisees, anyway? The word "pharisee" means the separated ones. They were the separatists. They were the people who refused to go the liberal way. They got their start as reactionists against the liberalism of their day. They believed in the literal application of the law of God. I do too. They believed in miracles. I do too. They believed in a literal Heaven and Hell. I do too. They believed in the resurrection. I do too. They believed in prayer and fasting. I do too. As far as I can find in the scriptures, the Pharisees are the original conservative movement who reacted against the liberalism of their time. But they crucified Jesus, because as they came down through the years, they became more and more strict in the outward things and neglected more and more the inner condition of their hearts until they finally lost any grace. They lived entirely in terms of external things.

Paul said, *"In the last days perilous times shall come. . . ."* and he lists the common sins. These people, he said, would have a form of godliness but deny the power thereof. Their religion will consist of a continuance of the outward form without the reality. Formalism can persist in the liberal circles, but formalism can prevail in the conservative circles just as easily. Anytime we begin to emphasize and accentuate the external to the neglect of the internal condition of our heart, we are in danger of hypocrisy. We have to have a balance of the inner heart relationship to God and the outer conformity to the will of God. If we neglect either, we can go into hypocrisy and be lost.

Another area of hypocrisy was the condemnation of others for these little details while neglecting the far more important issues in their own lives. In Matthew chapter seven, Jesus speaks of those who pick little motes out of the eyes of somebody else and neglect the great big beams in their own life—the people who use spy-glasses and look with an eagle gaze on somebody, sizing him up to see if they can find something to condemn in that person while neglecting a far more vast area of need in their own lives. "Woe to you hypocrites! Take the beam out of your own eye, then you can help your brother get that tiny little speck out of his life." Jesus was very specific. He said, "You tithe of mint and anise and cummin. If you have ten radishes, you would count out nine for yourself and put one in the tithe. Every lettuce leaf you count out one by one; you're very meticulous." Then He said, "That's good, you should do this. But you are neglecting the far weightier issues in your life of righteousness and mercy and faith. You ought to do both. You ought to be careful in the details of your life, but you ought to be far more concerned about these vital issues in your life." Jesus was severe on this.

God save us from going the way the Pharisees went. We can become so overbalanced in looking at people externally. That's what we see first, and that's about all we're interested in. I know a church in a university town where the pastor had a heart of love. He was a well balanced preacher, a man who loved lost people. They were coming in, and they were being saved. In that congregation was a dear lady who would see these young converts looking just like the world. She would look them up and down and size them up, then she would go to them and say, "Would you give me your address, please?" She would call on them just as soon as she could get there and read all the rules to them: You've got to do this. You've got to take this off. You've got to put this on. You've got to stay away from this. You can't go here. You can't do that. The new converts soon left. Pharisee!

Jesus was very strict about this. You have no right to pick at the little things in the lives of others and neglect love and mercy and compassion and righteousness in your own heart. If you do, you're a Pharisee, a hypocrite. You're going in the wrong direction. Oh, how we need to show a fresh overflow of love in reaching out to those who are lost! We love you, lost people, we love you. We don't love your ways, but we love your souls. Can we show it? God help us.

The Love of Material Possessions Probed

Another area where Jesus was very strict was in regard to the love of material possessions. Here in chapter six, beginning in verse nineteen and all the rest of this chapter, He deals with this one issue. Almost one-sixth of His whole sermon deals with the danger of falling in love with our material possessions. *Lay not up for yourselves treasures upon earth, where moth and rust doth corrupt . . . for where your treasure is, there will your heart be also.* This was an emphasis He carried consistently clear through His ministry. He never varied from it.

He was teaching His disciples when He told about the rich farmer who tore down his barns and built greater, saying to himself, *Soul, soul, thou hast much goods laid up for many years; take thine ease, eat, drink, and be merry.* God said, *Thou fool, this day shalt thy soul be required of thee.* Anybody who is accumulating the things of this world but isn't rich toward God, Jesus said, is a fool.

We have the record of the rich young ruler who came to Jesus, saying, *Master, what good thing shall I do, that I may have eternal life?* Jesus said, *Sell that thou hast, and give to the poor, and come and follow me.* He turned away sorrowful, for he had many possessions. Jesus was narrow.

But that's not the end of it. Jesus said something similar about you and me in the Gospel of Luke. Again there were great multitudes following after Him, and Jesus said, *If any man come to me, and hate not his father, and mother, and wife, and children, and brethren, and sisters, yea, and his own life also, he cannot be my disciple.. . . . So likewise, whosoever he be of you that forsaketh not all that he hath, he cannot be my disciple.* If you are not willing to give up everything to follow Jesus, you'll not be a follower of Jesus Christ. That's the teaching of the Lord Jesus Christ.

Most of us do not have the faintest concept of what the love of possessions is doing to us, how much we are being hypnotized, anesthetized, by our affluence. There's far more materialism in the conservative holiness ranks than we would like to admit.

I have tried hard to recall every kind of toy that I had when I was a boy. I can remember that I had an old metal box—it was old before I ever got it—full of wooden alphabet blocks, and they were old before I ever got them. I played for hours with those alphabet blocks— that is about all I had at that time. I did have one little blue metal car which lasted until I was in high school. I had one little red wagon and one little sled which my father made out in the work house. I think I may have had a doll of my own at one time, too, or maybe I just took it away from my sister. I can't be sure about that. That was all I had! But you go into most of our homes today there are toy trains and toy airplanes and toy tanks and toy guns and dolls and stuff and stuff and stuff. There are boxes overflowing and toys under the bed and in the closet until you have to have a special room. The children play with a new toy for about a month and then have to have something new, so we give it to them.

We are doing something to the character of our young people by this practice. We are indoctrinating them to demand novelty in order to be interested. That's exactly why a lot of people sit in this meeting right here and say "I couldn't care less what you're saying, Preacher. I want something funny. I want something novel. I want something that excites me. You can't just talk to us and keep our interest. We've got to have toys. We've got to have chatter and laughter."

We are indoctrinating a group of young people who do not like to sit and think. I can remember the hours as a boy that I spent just thinking about eternity, about God, about Heaven, and about Hell, and the mighty impact such practice had on my life. We have so many radios and record players and TVs and all other kinds of noise makers that we are not developing thinkers. We are developing players with toys. Our kids have been brought up to demand excitement, not to think. Unless we can do something to shake off the paralysis of this kind of materialism, we're on a downward slide, and we'll never get off unless, by the help of God, we can shake this materialistic attachment. There are not very many homes today where children are being brought up as candidates for a mission field, where they are learning to eat things they don't like the taste of, where thy are learning to make real sacrifices for the good of somebody else, where they are learning the joy of giving up something they want to help somebody who doesn't have anything. I'm talking even about our holiness homes. In most of our homes, we just give the children what they want. I know we have to be careful where we draw the line, but brethren, we had better draw the line somewhere.

Another area where I think we ought to each draw a line relates to eating. God's Word has much to say about the sin of overeating and gluttony. We also ought to each draw a line to determine how much money we salt away to draw interest and how much money we put into a missionary cause.

Let's apply this now to our own teaching. How narrow should we be? Are we justified in being more narrow than Jesus? Are we justified in being more broad than Jesus? Or should we try to be just as narrow as He is? Well, I want to be just as narrow as Jesus is, no more, no less. I want to be like Him. I have chosen a couple of areas that I want to deal with if we have time.

I pointed out some areas that Jesus did emphasize, and, if we're true to Jesus, we must keep on emphasizing these three things. Can we go beyond it? Well, here's one thing He said before He went away, *I have yet many things to say unto you, but ye cannot bear them now. Howbeit when he, the Spirit of truth, is come, he will guide you into all truth: for he shall not speak of himself; but whatsoever he shall hear, that shall he speak: and he will shew you things to come* (John 16:12, 13). Jesus said there were many things He wanted to teach, but His disciples couldn't bear them yet. He did say, however, that the Holy Spirit would take the truth of God and apply it. In other words, Jesus was saying there are areas and issues in which the Holy Spirit will guide, issues to be dealt with in the future that He did not specifically deal with.

Paul illustrated this. He got into some areas that Jesus never once alluded to as an issue at all. I'll give you one example, that of circumcision. Jesus never had one thing to say about whether people ought to be circumcised. But Paul said, *Behold, I Paul say unto you, that if ye be circumcised, Christ shall profit you nothing* (Gal. 5:2). That's being pretty narrow. Now if I were to preach that in this camp meeting you probably would order me out. And you ought to, because it is not an issue today. But it was a real issue in Paul's day when Jews and Gentiles were being converted together and the Jews were insisting that the Gentiles had to come by way of Jewish circumcision to be Christians. Paul said, "If you do it, Christ profits you nothing." This was not an issue when Jesus was teaching because He was strictly among the Jews.

What am I saying? I am saying that the Holy Spirit will guide people to make application of the truth as the situation demands. That's why we need the Holy Spirit. Let me say something else. Paul taught this way by showing from the scriptures that he was justified in taking this position. He didn't say, "This is the way I think it ought to be, fellows." If Paul was speaking out of his own ideas, he admitted it frankly. But he drew his rules from the Word of God.

I praise God that His truth is of this nature, that it can be applied to any moral issue in any age. Aren't you glad for that out of the Word of God? We do not need to just pop up and say, "This is what I think, men. It's got to be like I see it or I can't have any fellowship." There is no basis whatsoever for taking that kind of a position. If we can't take the eternal word of God and make it apply to the issues of today, then we had better stay quiet and follow out our own personal convictions. If we cannot back it up with a "thus saith the Lord," if we cannot derive an application of scriptural principles to our particular situation, we had better let God direct each person individually. Isn't that safe? There are some people who seem to feel that the best thing we could possibly do is just to be as strict as we possibly can on every single issue. That's not Biblical. It's unbiblical. Jesus said about the scribes and Pharisees, "You heap grievous burdens on people that they find very heavy to bear." If we're so conservative as to say, "Well, praise God, if it's heavy to bear, that means it's right," we are being pharisaical.

In Acts, chapter fifteen, we have these words, *For it seemed good to the Holy Ghost, and to us, to lay upon you no greater burden than these necessary things.* The Holy Spirit doesn't want you to bear one burden that isn't necessary for you to bear. There is no virtue in laying on extra heavy burdens because that's the way to be old fashioned. That's the way to be pharisaical. There is no virtue in getting out our spy glasses and focusing on smaller and smaller issues and coming up with more sensational restrictions. The Holy Spirit tells us not to lay one thing upon you that isn't necessary. That's the guidance of the Holy Spirit. I want to stay exactly where the Holy Spirit is leading. I want to apply what He says to apply, but I don't want to apply one ounce of extra weight to people beyond what is necessary for them to bear.

There are some Bible standards. There are some scriptural applications for today. In the time that I have left I want to make application in a couple of areas. Did Jesus say anything about clothing? He certainly did. Let me read it to you. Mark twelve, thirty-eight: *Beware of the Scribes, which love to go in long clothing.* He did teach about clothing. There it is. That's about all of His teaching on clothing that I can find. What are you trying to say, Bro. Yocum? I am trying to illustrate that situations change. Jesus didn't have the problem of mini skirts or culottes or bikinis. Jesus had the problem of people who loved to wear long clothing. That illustrates precisely what I am talking about. Situations change. But the Word of God can be applied, and we ought to rightly divide the word of truth. We ought to find out what the Bible has to say and apply it. If it doesn't have an application, we should stay quiet.

Half-nudity was no problem in Jesus' day. It was no problem in St. Paul's day. It was no problem in the Old Testament. I have searched the whole Bible carefully to try to find a single instance where a woman put on a half-nude apparel in order to entice a man, and I don't find a single instance anywhere. Not one. Even the harlots, the prostitutes of that day, were well-covered, including their face. Nudity was considered so utterly shameful in Bible days that even a prostitute who wanted to entice men for her living would not uncover herself. I won't take time to read Isaiah chapter forty-seven, the first five verses, but there a woman is subjected to nudity to the thighs as a public punishment for her sin.

I believe fully with many commentators that in the beginning Adam and Eve were covered with garments of light. The glory of God's brightness enshrouded them. They didn't need clothing. In the Bible, glory and clothing are united, and shame and nakedness are united. The clothing we wear is God's ordained substitute for the lost glory. Nudity is a symbol of that lost glory. And how we dress is an expression of our appreciation of the glory of God. Do I have scripture for that? I certainly do. *Thou shalt make holy garments for Aaron thy brother, for glory and for beauty.* Clothing is a representation of the glory of God. When Adam and Eve sinned, they made for themselves aprons out of fig leaves. When God found them, one of the first things He did was to destroy their aprons and give them coats to cover them. The difference between an apron and a coat is in the covering it provides. Yes, I know there was a difference between fig leaves and skin. I know the symbolism of that, but the actual fact was that God would wanted them covered. That was true when there were only two people alive on the face of the earth, and they were man and wife in the presence of God. If it was true then, and if the people who crucified Jesus stripped Him to expose Him and humiliate Him and degrade Him in public, then can you and I appear half-nude in public and still be exalting and representing the glory of God? Absolutely not!

I'm taking this thing back to scripture. We have a right to speak in this area because the Bible has some very sacred truths to present to us. People who have this tendency to unclothe themselves to appeal to the opposite sex and appeal to the world have no conception of the glory of God and very little love, if any, for Him. The Bible has something to say in this area.

Let's take this matter of the confusion of the sexes. The passage of scripture is Deuteronomy twenty-two, verse five. *The woman shall not wear that which pertaineth unto a man, neither shall a man put on a woman's garment: for all that do so are an abomination unto the Lord thy God.* Now here's a principle that runs right through the Word of God. *We shall not confuse the sexes.* God made them man and woman, male and female, and they're to be kept that way from beginning to end. Repeatedly the Word warns against this effort to remove the lines of distinction. It applies in hair, it applies in dress, it applies in the place that we occupy, it applies in our responsibilities, and in other areas. Paul says in First Corinthians six, verse nine, that neither the effeminate, nor the abusers of themselves with mankind shall inherit the kingdom of God. Who are the effeminate? Men who want to act like women. Who are the abusers of themselves with mankind? The homosexuals. They leave off the proper relationship, abandon it for something of their own choosing.

What does "pertaineth to a man" mean? Does it mean you can't wear something that a man has worn? Something that was made specifically *for* a man? Or something that *looks* like a man? So far as I can find out, and I have asked Hebrew teachers, it means just this: "that which pertaineth to a man." That's probably broad enough to include all of these. At least it does mean that which looks like a man, that which breaks down the distinction between what a man should look like and what a woman should look like.

The word "abomination" here is a very strong term. There are two different words that are translated abomination in the King James Version. The one that is used here involves extremely serious issues that will always be issues in the mind of God. Let me give you some of the common instances. Homosexuality is one of them which God says is an abomination. So are all things related to idolatry: the making of graven images, a falling down to them, offering your children to the images, enticing other people. Paying your vows to God with the price of a harlot is an abomination. Abomination, relates to things that God will always hate.

You say, "What is it that pertains to a man?" Well, here is one mark of conservative people. If they are not exactly sure, they would rather stay on the safe side than to err on the dangerous side. When you come to an area of abomination, you are in a dangerous area, an area where we'd better be careful than to be careless.

I want to say three things before I pass from this issue. Consider the matter of history. How did this get started anyway? It got started in our defense plants when women put on the clothing of a man in order to do the work of a man.

Consider the matter of fashion. I was listening some time ago to a fashion expert. Not a Christian teacher, a fashion expert talking on the radio who called the popular styles of pants and slacks for women "mannish items of apparel." The fashion experts know that these are developed to be mannish. They pertain to a man.

Consider the matter of custom. You can go to an airport in any part of the world and there will be two restrooms: one with a figure in pants, and one with a figure in a dress. I have never yet seen a woman come up and say, "Which one pertains to a woman and which pertains to a man?" People all around the world know what it means. They know where to go in.

The last issue I'm going to talk about is that of hair. Paul, in First Corinthians, chapter eleven, speaks about hair in the matter of shame and glory. If a woman has long hair it is a glory to her. If a man has long hair it's a shame unto him. Now that is serious business. You are talking about shame and glory. In fact, Paul relates this to issues that are as current as today: to divine order, to creation, to the angels, to nature, and Glory.

God's established order is God first, then the Son, then the man, and then the woman. And He relates the issue of women's hair to this order.

The order of Creation relates to the issue of hair. God created man first, then the woman. That's just as true today as it was in the days of Corinth.

Women around the world have worn their hair long until Westerners introduced their worldliness. Did Jesus have anything to say about this? He certainly did. He went into the home of a Pharisee and a woman named Mary washed His feet with her tears. Jesus said to Simon, "Simon, this woman has dried my feet with her hair. She's a terrible sinner, but this woman has long enough hair to dry her feet." What am I saying? Women instinctually knew they should wear their hair long.

Paul declared plainly that it is a shame for a woman to either shear or shave her head. "Shear" means to cut some of one's hair; "shave" means to cut off all one's hair.

Let me close with one passage from Revelation 9:8 that speaks about a hoard of warriors who appear during the tribulation to inflict plagues upon mankind. *Their faces were as the faces of men. And they had hair as the hair of women.* From where did these people come? They came right out of hell, led by Apollyon, the prince of demons. It's amazing that the closer we get to the tribulation the more we see of people who look like this.

I don't want to be identified with that crowd, do you? I want to be identified with the followers of the Lamb! Jesus himself said that many are going in at the broad way, and few are going in at the narrow way. If you're following the multitude, the popular opinion, you're on the broad road going to destruction.

Let's get on the narrow way and stay there! Let's also win as many other souls to the narrow way and stay there all the way to Glory!

P****ASSIVE**** ****AND****
P****ASSIONATE**** ****P****EOPLE

*If your decisions are made in the light of God's
glory and His counsel, they are right, no matter
how many people would disapprove.*

We'll be looking at a portion of scripture that vividly
contrasts the life of Abraham with that of Lot. This passage
follows right after the battle that Abram had with the alliance
of four kings under the leadership of Chedorlaomer, the king
of Elam. This alliance of kings overwhelmed the whole city of
Sodom and took them captive. Although he was vastly out-
numbered, Abram rose up, went and did battle, overcame
this alliance of four kings, and delivered his nephew, Lot, his
family, and the other persons of Sodom. Abram won a
mighty victory through the intervention of God and brought
back all the captive souls and the goods of the city of Sodom.
I'll begin the reading in Genesis 14:13.

*And there came one that had escaped, and told
Abram the Hebrew; for he dwelt in the plain of Mamre the
Amorite, brother of Eshcol, and brother of Aner: and these
were confederate with Abram. And when Abram heard that
his brother was taken captive, he armed his trained servants, born in his own house, three hundred and eighteen,*

and pursued them unto Dan. And he divided himself against them, he and his servants, by night, and smote them, and pursued them unto Hobah, which is on the left hand of Damascus. And he brought back all the goods, and also brought again his brother Lot, and his goods, and the women also, and the people.

And the king of Sodom went out to meet him, after his return from the slaughter of Chedorlaomer and of the kings that were with him, at the valley of Shaveh, which is the king's dale. And Melchizedek king of Salem brought forth bread and wine: and he was the priest of the most high God. And he blessed him and said, Blessed be Abram of the most high God, possessor of heaven and earth: and blessed be the most high God, which hath delivered thine enemies into thy hand. And he gave him tithes of all. And the king of Sodom said unto Abram, Give me the persons, and take the goods to thyself. And Abram said to the king of Sodom, I have lifted up mine hand unto the Lord, the most high God, the possessor of heaven and earth, that I will not take from a thread even to a shoe-latchet, and I will not take any thing that is thine, lest thou shouldest say, I have made Abram rich: save only that which the young men have eaten, and the portion of the men which went with me, Aner, Eshcol, and Mamre; let them take their portion.

Genesis 14:13-24

I'm adding one verse as a text from Romans 12:21: *Be not overcome of evil, but overcome evil with good.*

This story represents two kinds of men, one passive, and one passionate. The passive person is pushed around by circumstances. He is tossed to and fro by any wind that blows. He is moved from one position to another by shifting opinion, shifting pressures, and shifting temptations. Wherever it's easiest to be, that's where you'll find him. Lot represents the passive person.

The passionate person stands like a Gibraltar, no matter from where the tide or the wind or the wave comes. He chooses the right course, even though circumstances may be against him. Abraham represents the passionate person.

It is said that one of Napoleon's generals came to him and asked, "Sir, what shall we do under these circumstances?"

"Under the *circumstances*?" Napoleon replied. "We make our own circumstances." I like that kind of spirit. If we are linked with almighty God, we are not moved by circumstances, no matter what the moral and spiritual condition of our age. We are anchored, and we overcome.

I want to consider some of the forces that acted on both Abram and Lot and note with you the different ways in which these men responded.

The Appeal of Earthly Things

Both Abram and Lot at times had great quantities of flocks, herds, and earthly possessions. They both knew the value of having these things, but they responded to this appeal in different ways. Lot represents a person who is attracted and drawn after earthly things to his own hurt, if not total destruction. He came out with Abram from Ur of the Chaldees and somewhat later from Haran. He followed along with Abram into the land of promise. God had assured Abram that He would give this land to him and his seed, but there came a point where Abram gave Lot a choice, and Lot lifted up his eyes and looked toward the valley of the Jordan. Without a tear, without a prayer, without asking for divine counsel, Lot chose after the sight of the eyes. He didn't ask what would be good in the long run for his spiritual welfare and the welfare of his children. He didn't ask what it was that God would have him do. He moved with his family in the direction of increasing material prosperity with apparently no concern about what the consequences might be for his spiritual condition. A great many people have done this. Abram didn't, and this marked the difference between him and Lot.

We all feel the pressure and the pull of material things. We live in a world where we have to pay taxes, buy our groceries, drive our automobiles, and heat our homes. We know the pressures that are upon us. These pressures can do awful things to us if we, like Lot, do not cast up a bulwark of resistance against the appeal and the pull of earthly things. The sin is not in possessing things. The sin, the danger, is in letting things possess us. It wasn't a demon that seduced Lot; it was exactly the same kind of pressure and appeal that we face almost every day.

Is there anybody here who is not feeling any pressure from the economic condition? Is there anybody here who is never bothered by the increasing price of gas or a loaf of bread? I don't think so. We all live in a world of this kind. As I've said before, I wouldn't be able to draw a specific line in outward circumstances between using this world and abusing this world. However, I do have to draw a line in my own heart, and so do you. We must be perfectly sure at all times that while we are using the things of this world, we are not abusing them—that is, while we are living in a world of material concerns, we are not allowing the concerns to overwhelm us in our spiritual life.

The Bible has a lot to say about this; Jesus taught much about the danger of allowing the pressure of earthly things to creep subtly in and get a throttling grasp upon our hearts. Paul wrote in I Timothy 6:8: *And having food and raiment, let us be therewith content.* Paul believed in being careful and making adequate provisions for our household. In fact, he said that if we were not doing that, we were worse than infidels and had denied the faith. But having said that, he said, *Having food and raiment, let us be therewith content. But they that will be rich* [not who *are* rich, but who have set their minds to *become* rich] *fall into temptations and a snare, and into many foolish and hurtful lusts, which drown men in destruction and perdition. For the love of money* [not money itself] *is the root of all evil: which while some coveted after, they have erred from the faith, and pierced themselves through with many sorrows.*

Notice the figures that he used here. He talked about this desire for wealth as pulling people under until they can't get their spiritual breath and die from drowning. He talked about people who pierce themselves through, a kind of suicide, if you please, because they desire more and more and more of the things of this world until their spiritual life is gone.

Jesus gave the parable of the sower and talked about the seed that fell among thorns. The thorns sprang up and choked the seed. He said that this represents those who, because of the cares and riches and pleasures of this world, bring no fruit to perfection but are choked.

Drowning. Piercing. Choking—all hard ways to die. We die spiritually when our care moves to riches and then to pleasures. I've seen this happen many, many times. Jesus warned against this. There are times when people can't make ends meet, then they accumulate some riches and not only can make ends meet but also have some extra money. Do they say, "Praise God, I can put every penny of it into a missionary offering"? Sadly, many times they don't. They say, "I've got extra; now I can buy tickets to a football game." That's extremely dangerous ground. I'm really concerned about people who have enough that they can fulfill any desire whether it's Godly or not. Jesus said that riches choke people until they don't bring any fruit to perfection. They are fruitless.

I've seen so many examples of this. I think about a man who was called to preach, but World War II broke out at that time and he got a job in a defense plant where the income was greater than he had ever known before. He wasn't able to give the money up and pay tuition to go to Bible college. It was so much more comfortable to have money coming in than having it going out for a Bible college education. He never made it into the ministry. The snare of riches pulled him under and drowned him.

Riches appealed to Lot. He was drawn along in the direction of the greenest fields and the most prosperous city to live in. He didn't settle it for God; he settled it for the sight of his eyes. Oh friends, how many people are going that way! How many don't stop to consider the consequences and pray their decision through. What is the best for our spiritual interests? There is a higher paying job over here, although there's no holiness church, no Christian school. Off they trot. What happens to them? Just what happened to Lot. They are pulled under and drowned. There are far higher considerations than where you can get the next promotion or the next advance in your pay.

Abram wasn't that way. Abram felt the appeal, but he had some firm resolutions in his life. We recognize it here in chapter fourteen in a very thrilling story. Abram's flocks and herds were multiplying, especially when he won this battle over four kings who had taken captive all the people and all the goods of the city of Sodom. Since Abram won the battle, he had the right to take all of those people captive as his slaves, and all of the goods to be his personal treasures. Have you ever dreamed about something like that? I've dreamed about coming upon a chest of gold spilling out where I could just shovel it up! Here Abram wins a mighty battle by the help of the Lord, and all of the goods of the big and prosperous city of Sodom fall into his lap, as it were. Sodom was noted for, among other things, plenty of bread, plenty of material things, and love of ease. And it was all Abram's!

What did Abram do with all this great store that poured in upon him? Well, the first thing he did when he met Melchizedek was pay his tithe. That's a good rule to follow. Melchizedek blessed him and said, "Abram, God gave this to you. God helped you to get this." Abram said, "All right, let's pay the tithes."

Then he met the king of Sodom who said, "I'll make a deal with you, Abram. You give me all the people that you have taken captive, let me take them back to Sodom, and I will give you all the goods." Abram said, "I have raised up my hand to God, the possessor of heaven and earth. My God owns everything. I'm not even going to take a piece of thread or a shoe string. I'm not going to have anybody saying that the king of Sodom made me rich. If God wants to make me rich, well and good, but I'll not take the wealth from Sodom." He did this because he wanted to keep his word. "I made a pledge before God, saying I will not take a thread out of this. I'll just trust the Lord." Isn't that great? That's the difference between Lot and Abram. One of them is moved by the appeal of Sodom and then loses everything. The other is moved by the appeal of God and gains everything He wants to give him.

The Stress on Heavenly Things

The appeal of earthly things and the stress on heavenly things are related. A person who is attracted by earthly things will not sense that high attraction of heavenly things. You can't serve two masters. You will either love the one and hate the other or you will cling to one and despise the other. Lot represents a person who followed after the things of God for a while but was not consistent and committed.

Look at the two of them in regard to the altars of God. The Bible doesn't say anything about Lot building an altar. He was there when God spoke to Abram, but God never spoke to Lot. He had a second generation religion.

This religion really meant something to Abram. It was firsthand with him. He had some face-to-face encounters with God, and they were more precious than anything else in the world to him. Lot was there and sensed something was going on when the God of glory appeared to Father Abram and talked to him face to face, but Lot never experienced God himself.

I want to speak to some of you young people here. I beg of you, don't just go on depending on your parents' encounters with God. Anybody who can understand what I am saying right now is old enough to begin to have some of his or her own personal encounters with God. That's right.

Some encounters I had with God as a youth are still as vivid in my memory as if they happened yesterday. They happened long before I was ten years of age—even before I was seven years of age. Thank God, children, if your parents have an altar that you can attend. Thank God for the church where you can attend and sense those precious times of God's glorious manifestations. There is no way of putting a value on these manifestations of God's glorious presence. However, it's one thing to look on as you recognize that God is in this place, and it's another thing to engage your own heart and be a part of it. It's unspeakably important in your life to have a place where it's not just Dad and Mother getting blessed and enjoying God but where you enjoy God. God wants that to be true. I say it again, any child who can understand what I'm saying is old enough to begin to have some personal experiences with the almighty God that help tie you down and get your roots fixed until you'll not move around by every wind of doctrine. Oh, I thank God for that!

I enlisted in the Air Force even before the outbreak of World War II and was sent to the Massachusetts Institute of Technology to study meteorology. I still remember the first night I arrived in Boston. I stayed in an old, second-rate hotel. I spent a long time alone with God there that evening, away from home, away from my home church. This would have been a real opportunity to tour Boston, but I didn't want to go out and see the town. I wanted to see God. I wanted a fresh visitation of God on my soul. I still remember the sacred hours in that hotel room that evening with the presence of God revealed to my soul and the assurance that wherever duty might call me to go, God would go along and be the preserver of my soul. Oh, praise God. It wasn't Dad and Mother's altar then. It was my own personal altar.

God never forsook me in all of those years when I was going to various parts of the world in military service. There were furious temptations, and others were falling on the right and on the left to sensuality, to sin, and to shame, but God held me in check. He kept His hand upon me. There had been an altar in an old hotel room.

Lot never built that kind of altar. He got away from the altars that Abram had built and went his own way. What a tragedy! I talked to a mother in North Carolina a few years ago who told of her son who had been raised around the family altar. She heard a ruckus from his room one day and went upstairs and asked, "Son, what's the matter up here?" He said, "Mom, I'm not going that way!" She said, "What do you mean? Why?" He picked up the Bible and threw it against the wall and said, "I'm through. I'm not going that way." He didn't. He went out and got into drugs, joined a hippie commune and all the rest that goes along with it. Weeping, she asked, "What can I do?"

Well, a man has the power of choice. Lot did, and this son did. He only stayed around his mother's altar until he got big enough to assert his own authority and go his own way. I hope our children don't do that. That's a real danger unless God reveals to their own hearts that He is great enough for their generation as well as their parents' generation. And He is! Praise the Lord!

Abram was passionate about the altars. The greatest things that happened in Abram's life happened around his altars. The decisions that Abram made in the light of God's fresh revelation were wise decisions no matter how foolish they looked. The decisions he made away from the altars of revelation were foolish decisions no matter how wise they looked.

Let's review a few of these decisions. Whoever would have called it a wise move to leave Ur of the Chaldees where he was well-fixed and well-settled and go to a place he knew nothing of? Why, that would have been the sheerest folly if God had not been leading. It was the right decision, however, because the God of glory spoke to him and led him out. Who would think wise the decision to take his firstborn son Ishmael and turn him out of his own house, not knowing where he would go? It was a wise decision because he got it in the light of God's personal counsel. Whoever would endorse the decision to take his second son, Isaac, go to the top of a mountain, bind him on an altar of sacrifice, and burn him to death? Nobody would ever second the motion to that, but it was wise because the decision was made in the light of God's counsel.

I'll tell you something, dear people, it doesn't matter how foolish your decision looks in the eyes of the world. If it's made in the light of God's glory and His counsel, it's right no matter how many people would disapprove of it.

Look at those decisions Abraham made that were not decided at the altar or in the light of God's glory. He decided to go down into Egypt when a famine came. The world is still reaping the horrible consequences of that miscalculation in high gas and oil prices. However, that decision is one that people would have seconded. "Why sure, if it's dry around here, if there's a famine here and things are green down in the Nile Valley, go on down there, of course." But this decision wasn't made in the light of God's counsel, and it was wrong, dead wrong.

There was the decision that his wife suggested to him. "I'm too old to bear a son. Take Hagar and have a son." That sounded reasonable enough for Abraham to accept, but it was wrong, dead wrong, and we are still paying the price for that.

Let me apply this. There are multitudes of people who are making key decisions about their lives out of the context of God's revealed glory. They are making decision in the light of some popular opinion of the world, some counsel of people who are not spiritually discerning. They are making lifetime decisions without a revelation of God's glory or a voice of His own personal counsel. They are foolish! They are dead wrong!

I remember talking to a young lady who was compromising. She was giving all of her reasons. "Where I work, I'm too conservative for them. They disdain me." She was doing some things to fit in. I said, "Have you really prayed about this to find out what pleases God?" "No," she said, "I haven't." She went on that way. Her home was broken. She fell into deep, deep immorality. She didn't pray about her decisions. She leaned to her own understanding and went wrong. We can't afford to make key decisions without a manifestation of God's presence and his direction in our life.

Abram treasured these times at the altar. How much they meant to him! He made great spiritual development around the altar. Lot went downward. Abram went upward. Lot first went into the plain of the Jordan. Later, he moved into the city of Sodom. He changed his tent for a strong dwelling house with doors that would lock. He was a judge in the city of Sodom. That's progress, isn't it, to go from being a farmer living around barren hills in an old tent and move into a strong house in a lavish, lush green valley. People in the city bowed down before Lot. But not everything that looks like progress in the eyes of the world is progress in the eyes of God. Lot became insensitive to what was happening to him. He moved along before the tide of circumstances. Material circumstances crowded out spiritual considerations in his life.

This process of cooling off happened to the Laodiceans. "Thou art lukewarm. I want you to be zealous," Jesus said. But they weren't. Jesus said that because iniquity shall abound, the love of many shall wax cold. That's not a sudden sharp drop in temperature. It's a gradual, subtle, process that is almost impossible to discern without spiritual insight. People will be passive while experiencing the cooling off process.

Consider the ground squirrels. They are cold-blooded, and whatever happens to the temperature around them, happens to them. When it gets colder, the squirrels slow down. They may crawl into a hollow log or under some piles of wood. When the temperature drops, they lose all consciousness of what's going on around them. Their temperatures can fall virtually to the freezing level. They're not dead; they're hibernating. They are totally unconscious of anything going on around them. You wouldn't dare to warm them up too quickly. They would die. Revival has to come slowly to some people. They couldn't stand the full blaze of a Holy Ghost revival until they started to come back from the verge of death.

That's not what the tree squirrel does. The tree squirrel is warm-blooded. Did you ever see a tree squirrel when it gets cold? The squirrel is out there looking for nuts. His feet get cold, and he smacks them together. He runs up a tree, bounces around, and flips his tail in the air; he's fighting off the cold. He's not about to just sit on a log and be overcome with the cold. *Be not overcome with evil, but overcome evil with good.* Be not overcome by the cold, but overcome the cold by some spiritual exercises.

We have two instruments on this wall. One of them is a thermometer, and the other is a thermostat. The thermometer simply tells us what is happening but has no capacity to do a thing about it. When the temperature drops, the indicator on the thermometer drops. If the temperature rises, it rises. The thermostat is different. It not only reacts to what is happening but it changes what is happening. It overcomes the circumstances. Which are you? Are you a thermometer who simply registers how cold it is, or are you a thermostat who reverses the course of things. We've got to have revival here. Amen?

Lot had some children in the city of Sodom. They got adjusted to city living. I suppose they heard about Abram, and maybe there were times when they visited him, but the girls in Sodom had their opinion of that bearded mountaineer who still thought he's going to have a son. I'm sure that they made a mockery of old Uncle Abram. Well, they can thank Abram for their life. Sodom wouldn't have been spared if it had been left up to Lot and his family. There was a man up in the mountains who knew how to pray, who knew how to fight off the cold, who knew how to get hold of God. He prayed and God said, "Yes, if there are ten righteous here, I will spare the city." Abram had audience with the Holy One. He had access to the Almighty. The Bible says that God remembered Abram. He knew the place where he stood up on the mountain when he prayed and overlooked this wicked city. Because of that praying man, Lot and his family were delivered out of Sodom when it was destroyed by fire.

What is our power in prayer? We as parents have some mighty serious responsibilities in praying for our sons and our daughters, our nieces and our nephews. Abram wasn't praying for his son; he was praying for a nephew and his family. He was interceding, and God remembered Abram and brought Lot and his family out. I believe we as parents have the right to have an intercession with God, an encounter with God, on behalf of our children and their spiritual welfare. Praise the Lord for the privilege.

Lot needed a radical transformation in his life. If I had only the New Testament to go by, I would consider that Lot made it to heaven. If I had only the Old Testament to go by, I would consider that Lot lost his soul. As it is, I'm not really sure, but I'm very, very fearful that Lot missed it. The New Testament said that he vexed his righteous soul from day to day by the wickedness of the people around him. One of the meanings of the word "vexed" is "to wear out." I think that's what happened to Lot. When he first went into the city of Sodom and saw the immorality, the bestiality, of these awful people, his soul was horrified. But he didn't get out. He stayed in. His wife liked it there. His daughters liked it there. While he protested, he didn't really do anything about it. He gradually wore down his protest, wore down his resistance. He never declared an emergency and had a real spiritual reversal in his life. He's a passive person.

There was a time when the angels of God came into Sodom and came to Lot's door. The men of the city came and tried to abuse these visitors. Lot was so polite, so diplomatic, saying, "Oh, my good friends, my dear neighbors, don't be ungracious to these visitors. I'll give you my daughters." Can you imagine this business man bartering away his own daughters to these beasts because he doesn't want to declare a protest against this evil in the city? We don't have to give the gay rights movement a place in government, in our schools. Not if we have a conscience. Not if we have a soul. What a compromise Lot made! What spiritual loss! These angels pulled him inside and struck the men with blindness.

The angels of God said, "Do you have any loved ones in this town? You better tell them this city is going to be destroyed." Lot the diplomat crosses town to where his sons-in-law live. "Now gentlemen, I don't like to do anything precipitously, but I do have word that the welfare of this city is at stake and we might be well advised to evacuate the city until the storm is over."

I read this passage in Scripture many times before I grasped what it really says. Every time I read this I thought that his sons-in-law mocked him, but that's not what it says. It says that he was to them as one who mocked. His suave diplomacy about handling emergency situations never did persuade them that something serious was about to happen. They laughed right along. They thought he was just telling them a big joke. He went back home without his sons-in-law. I don't know how many daughters he lost in this city.

The angels said, "Look Lot, this city is going to be destroyed. If you don't get out of here and do it quickly, you'll be swallowed up." The diplomat speaks, "Well, let's not do anything hastily. I'm a judge in this city. The people are bound to ask questions if we just rush out of here like we're frightened." You know what the angel had to do? He had to take that family by the hand and actually pull them out of the city to save their lives. He told them to get out and get to the mountains, but Lot said, "Would you please let me stay in the city of Zoar?" The angel said, "All right, if that's what you want, you can go to Zoar," which means "little."

The next chapter in Lot's life story is a very sordid, very sad story indeed, the story of a drunken man involved in incest resulting in two sons who were the enemies of God's people. The curtain falls on the passive man. I have serious concern about his immortal soul. Lot's problem is the problem of a lot of other people who have gone the same way. They never stand up and say, "I've got to fight this cooling, chilling climate. I've got to have a personal revival in my life." They go the way Lot went. There are people all around us who need to declare a real emergency in their souls. "I'm cooling off. I'm just shifting about before circumstances, public opinions, and changing standards. I've got to get a fresh glimpse of God and a fresh encounter with heaven." We have to, friends. We've got to have it or be lost just like Lot was.

I'm not going to call you to a public altar. But it might be good for us all to just go home and have a family altar, a personal altar. Lord help us to withstand the cold, the encroaching spirit of the age, the spirit of diplomacy, the spirit of adjustment. Lord, help us be passionate Christians.

WHEN PRAYER SEEMS FUTILE

Why does God sometime seem deaf to our cry,
seem unmoved to our supplication, our most
intense times of prayer?

My text is found in Luke chapter twenty-two, beginning with verse thirty-nine.

*And when he came out, and went, as he was wont,
to the mount of Olives; and his disciples also followed him.
And when he was at the place, he said unto them, "Pray
that ye enter not into temptation." And he was withdrawn
from them about a stone's cast, and kneeled down, and
prayed, Saying, "Father, if thou be willing, remove this cup
from me: nevertheless not my will, but thine, be done."
And there appeared an angel unto him from heaven,
strengthening him. And being in an agony he prayed more
earnestly: and his sweat was as it were great drops of blood
falling down to the ground. And when he rose up from
prayer, and was come to his disciples, he found them sleep-
ing for sorrow, And said unto them, "Why sleep ye? rise
and pray, lest ye enter into temptation."*
*And while he yet spake, behold a multitude, and he
that was called Judas, one of the twelve, went before them,*

and drew near unto Jesus to kiss him. But Jesus said unto him, "Judas, betrayest thou the Son of man with a kiss?" When they which were about him saw what would follow, they said unto him, "Lord, shall we smite with the sword?"

And one of them smote the servant of the high priest, and cut off his right ear. And Jesus answered and said, "Suffer ye thus far." And he touched his ear, and healed him. Then Jesus said unto the chief priests, and captains of the temple, and the elders, which were come to him, "Be ye come out, as against a thief, with swords and staves? When I was daily with you in the temple, ye stretched forth no hands against me: but this is your hour, and the power of darkness."

I am speaking on the subject, "When Prayer Seems Futile." I would like to read verse forty-four again as a text:

And being in an agony he prayed more earnestly: and his sweat was as it were great drops of blood falling down to the ground.

In my estimation this is the most sacred, most intense, most significant hour of prayer in all of history. And yet, Jesus Christ, the Son of God, the eternal one, praying as intensely as He prayed, did not have His desire granted. He did not receive from His Father what he had hoped to receive in His prayer. His prayer appeared futile.

I am quite sure that any of us who have prayed in any measure of seriousness have been confronted with this apparent futility of our praying. It isn't doing any good. We prayed for God to heal; He didn't heal. We prayed for God to open doors; they remained closed. We prayed for God to save; He didn't save—at least so it appeared to us. If you have felt this way at any time, then you are identifying with many people, including some in Scripture, who have been earnest in prayer but didn't feel that God was hearing their prayer.

Some people, as a consequence of this, decreased the amount of their praying and turned to something which seemed to them to be more efficient than prayer. Many people have turned away from intense praying to an intensified human activity. That seems more efficient. We get things done. And praying just doesn't seem to pay.

Well, I've passed through times like this, and they haven't all been forty years ago, either. But I ask the question, "Why does God sometime seem deaf to our cry, seem unmoved to our supplication, our most intense times of prayer?"

Let me read to you from Psalm forty-four, verse twenty-three. The psalmist David cried out, *Awake, why sleepest thou, O Lord.* "Lord, I'm leading the battle, and You're sound asleep. Would you please wake up and pay attention to me?" He continues, *Arise, cast us not off for ever.* It seems like God is sound asleep and is paying no attention to the prayers of His people. So if you have felt that way, David makes good company.

Here are the words of Jeremiah, chapter fourteen, verse nine, praying. *Why shouldest thou be as a man astonied, as a mighty man that cannot save? yet thou, O Lord, are in the midst of us, and we are called by thy name; leave us not.* "Lord, we believe You're a mighty man, but it just looks like You can't save anybody."

Even Jesus on the cross prayed, *My God, my God, why hast thou forsaken me?* Jesus, here in the most intense season of prayer in all history, prayed, and it seemed like God wasn't hearing and wasn't answering. He was hearing, but it didn't seem like it. God wasn't asleep when David prayed that way, but it seemed like it. God was still able to save when Jeremiah prayed, but it seemed like He couldn't. So if you've been tempted that way, I say again, you're in good company.

What are some of the reasons why prayer seems futile at times? I certainly cannot treat all of the reasons—there are probably twenty-five or thirty specific reasons given in the scriptures why God doesn't answer some prayers. I'm not going through all of them, but I would just summarize here by saying one reason God doesn't answer prayer or why prayer seems futile is because the conditions for prayer are not being met.

MEETING THE CONDITIONS OF PRAYER

I want to examine the case of Jesus here in the light of some of the conditions of prayer. There are many. And surely one lesson that we all need to learn about prayer is that we do not take just one passage about prayer in isolation and treat it as if it summarized all the conditions of prayer. No single verse anywhere does that. There are conditions for prayer to be effective, and if our prayer is to be effective, then we must meet the conditions that are given in a number of passages about prayer.

There are laws of prayer I believe, beloved, that are just as definite as the laws of electricity. James said *The effectual fervent prayer of a righteous man availeth much*. The word "effectual" means to pray according to the conditions of prayer. That is not just some vague and meaningless word; it means to pray according to God's conditions of prayer. (Andrew Murray wrote a book entitled *With Christ in the School of Prayer*, a great book that is worth reading because it treats some of the conditions of effective praying.)

I don't know how you feel, but I want to know how to pray effectively. I want to be an achiever in prayer. One of the old worthies said, "The greatest of teachers would he be who could set the Church to praying." I think that's true.

Intensity

One of the conditions of prayer is the condition of intensity. Was Jesus meeting the condition of intensity in prayer? Oh yes, a thousand times yes. The text said, *Being in an agony, he prayed more earnestly: and his sweat was as it were great drops of blood...* The pressure that He was under, the strain of the burden that He bore, so compressed Him physically that it actually pressed the blood out through the pores of His body. The Hebrew writer said, *Ye have not yet resisted unto blood, striving against sin.* Do you know of anybody who has ever prayed that intensely, until the blood was dripping from his body like sweat? James said "The effectual, fervent. . . ." That means fiery hot in its intensity. That kind of praying availeth much, James says.

David Brainerd was one of the greatest prayer warriors in our American history. He went as a missionary to the American Indians, spending much time in the forests where the Indians were. He wrote a journal about his life, and one of the entries tells about a time when he was so under pressure of the lostness of these American Indians, that he fell on the ground at a time when there was snow and melted the snow away from his body by the perspiration of that intense day in prayer. Beyond the point where he had melted the snow, the snow had been spotted with the blood that he had coughed forth from his lungs because he had tuberculosis. He died at about the age of thirty and said, "I wish I had a thousand lives to give in a cause so glorious." That's intensity.

One of the episodes in the Welsh revival under the ministry of Evan Roberts was an occasion when F. B. Meyer and a friend of his visited the revival services. It was a great meeting. The place was crowded with people who had come to hear Evan Roberts preach and to see what God might do that day. In the service, a young man rose and said, "I am an agnostic. If God wants to save me, I'm going to give Him a fair opportunity. Let Him do it!" Evan Roberts took that as a real challenge. He dropped to his knees and began to groan and plead with God in prayer so intensely, and so protractedly that the friend of F. B. Meyer said, "I can't bear this groaning! I can't endure this awful groaning! I'm going to start a song and drown out this man." Meyers said, "Whatever you do, don't do that. I want the noise of these sobs to sink into my soul. I've been dry-eyed too long. Too long I have preached the gospel without any tears, without any groans."

Evan Roberts went on groaning and sobbing and pleading with God for some ten minutes. Then Roberts arose and addressed the young man. "Will you yield?" The man shot back, "Why should I yield?" This time Evan Roberts asked the whole congregation to join him in prayer. F. B. Meyers said that the place was so filled with the sighs and the groans and the sense of pressure that eventually F. B. Meyers rose to his feet, gasping almost for breath as if it would stifle him. Oh, the pressure of the burden on those weeping, sobbing, groaning, pleading people! He said, "Oh, God, let this sob sink itself into my soul. Let me never forget this noise of sobbing. Lord, enable me to sob over the lost souls of men."

For another extended period the congregation was groaning, moved like a forest before a mighty wind with the spirit of real intercession. Finally the young man broke and came and was saved. A lot of people today would consider this the rankest kind of fanaticism, but it is not.

People don't really apply prayer any more. It's too inefficient, too unappealing, too costly. There are lots of clever substitutes that look good to the carnal eye and seem good to a carnal evaluation. God places high premium on this kind of intensity. Look at Jesus. He's no fanatic. Paul said that the Holy Spirit is given to us for one thing—to make intercession for us with groanings that can not be uttered. That's not fanaticism. That's one of the designated ministries of the Holy Spirit in the lives of God's saints—to make praying intense enough that you can't even put it into words.

Take the occasion of Elijah on Mt. Carmel. After he had prayed down fire, he went on to the top of the mountain to pray for rain. He only prayed fifty-seven words and the fire fell. But when he got to the top of the mountain to pray for rain, it was a harder task. He cast himself on the ground. That sounds like a man who is doing violence in the place of prayer. He put his head between his knees and began to pray for rain. After a time of prayer, he sent his servant to look out over the horizon to see if there was any rain coming from out over the Mediterranean. The servant came back and said that there was none. The second time Elijah went down with his face to the ground between his knees pleading with God to send rain upon a thirsty land. Seven times over he did that.

Why did God let a servant of His, one who could pray down fire with fifty-seven words, go through this contortion of pressure and strain and groaning seven times before He put a little cloud there the size of a man's hand. Why? Couldn't God have done it after he mentioned it the first time? Oh, yes, He could have. Then why didn't He? Why does God keep people going back and putting their face on the ground seven times over before He gives a tiny little fragment of cloud? Is He grudging? Is He asleep? Is He on a long journey where He can't hear? No, absolutely not. I would suggest to you that God did that because He wanted to show a man as earnest as the occasion merited.

I would suggest that God doesn't answer many of our prayers because we haven't yet approached at all the measure of earnestness that the occasion merits. God wants us to have clarified vision. He wants us to be realistic. He wants us to have an intensity that is, at least in some measure, commensurate with the demand that's before us.

The Irish evangelist Roland Hill was a fiery preacher, a passionate evangelist. People had been charging him with mere enthusiasm. Preaching to the people of a small village, he said, "I want to tell you that I am not a man of mere enthusiasm." He continued, "Some years ago I stood on a hill over against this village. I was looking down into the streets and into this village, and as I watched I saw some of your children playing in a gravel pit, just outside this town. And as I watched, I saw the children playing in the gravel, and I saw a big slide of gravel come down and bury those children in the gravel pit.

"I knew there wasn't much time, and I raised my voice and screamed. I yelled until I aroused the people of this town and told them what was wrong, and nobody charged me with being too enthusiastic. Nobody came and said, 'That's nonsense. That's silly. That's out of place in a village as intelligent as this one is.'" But he said, "I am dealing with something far more serious today than three or four of your boys and girls being buried in a gravel pit. I'm dealing with your immortal souls going down to eternal torment. I'm not a mere enthusiast. I'm being serious because the problem is serious."

Again, I would suggest that one reason why God doesn't answer when we pray is that we're not yet as serious as the occasion really demands. I was with a father, a good godly man, at the bedside of a little lad who had spinal meningitis. The father was concerned because that's a deadly disease. I heard him say to the doctor, "Doctor, don't pay any attention to the cost. Whatever it takes to help my boy, don't stop to ask how much it will cost. I want him well." Is that fanaticism? No, that's not fanaticism. That's a love that a father has for his son.

Are we more concerned about the sickness of our son or daughter than we are about the lost souls of multitudes all around about us? Does God have to put a child of ours next to death physically before we act as seriously as we ought?

One Christian man had a son who came very close to death. The father was spending some sleepless hours in prayer before God to heal his boy. In those night hours the Lord began to deal with that father and said, "Your boy has been lost all these months, hasn't he?" The father said, "Yes." God said, "How many sleepless hours have you spent over his lost soul?" The father confessed, "None." The Lord said to him, "You're more concerned about a physical illness of your boy that threatens life than you are over his lost estate that threatens him to eternal damnation."

The father repented of his prayerlessness that night and spent more hours not just praying for the body of his son but for the souls of his four other children, all lost. Although he was the father of five children, he was not excited enough about their lost condition to lose one hour sleep until one of them became seriously ill. He prayed on, with increasing intensity, until God did hear and healed that boy. But more important, God saved those children, and they went on living for the Lord.

In the garden of Gethsemane, the disciples were not as serious as they ought to have been. Jesus was going into the garden of His agony. He had a greater agony there in the garden than He did on the cross, an anguish indescribably intense. He needed the support of His disciples. He said, "Would you watch with me? Watch with me for an hour?" He took His closest friends, Peter, James, and John. He brought them very near to His place of prayer and said, "You men watch with me here." He went on about a stone's throw farther and fell on His face and prayed the prayer that I have read. When He went back to them they were asleep. They were not watching with Him.

When a person has his eyes open and begins to realize the lostness of men and women around him, when a person gets a vision that drives him to his knees in intercessory prayer, it's hard to understand how people walking in the fellowship of believers can live with so little intensity.

If any of us could go behind the Iron Curtain and fellowship with praying people in Russia, China, or in some other countries much less endowed materially than we are, and if we should company with them for a few weeks and should sense the passion of their praying, the first thing that would strike us upon returning to American churches would be, "How can we American people be so casual when needs are so inexpressibly great and souls are so lost?"

Evangelist James A. Stewart ministered behind the Iron Curtain to people who were living under the rule of Communism. After coming to the United States and visiting some churches, he said, "I would rather spend my days in a

Russian prison camp than to spend them in most American churches. It's easier to be spiritual there than it is here." We have departed so far from a Biblical standard of intensity in prayer that such a position seems almost foreign to us. Who has resisted unto blood, striving in prayer against sin like Jesus did here? Who has sweat, as it were, great drops of blood?

Submissiveness to the Will of God

A second condition of prayer is submissiveness to the will of God. Jesus did submit Himself to the will of God. That's why His prayer was not granted, his request was denied. In every case, He said, *If it be possible, let this cup pass from me. Nevertheless, not my will, but thine be done.*

Jesus knew it was God's will for Him to die on the cross. He knew that's what He had come into the world to do. He had set His face to go to Jerusalem. He wasn't rebelling against the will of God; but neither was He anticipating the suffering of being a mortal man in a human frame who was going to endure the weight of all lost people of all ages. That's why He said, *Father, if thou be willing, remove this cup from me: nevertheless not my will, but thine, be done.* The suffering was all in the cup that He, as a mortal man, was to take in His body and bear to the place of death by crucifixion.

I don't wonder that every fiber of His being cried for deliverance, for release. "Oh, if it be possible, let this cup pass from me." But He knew what God's will was. A little bit later He said to the disciples, after Peter had smitten off the ear of Malchus, *Thinkest thou that I cannot now pray to my Father, and he shall presently give me more than twelve legions [thousands] of angels? But how then shall the scripture be fulfilled, that thus it must be?* (Matthew 26:53, 54). It must be. But He submitted Himself to the will of God. His prayer was heard.

In Hebrews, chapter five, verse seven, the writer says of this event, *Who in the days of his flesh, when he had offered up prayers and supplications with strong crying and tears unto him that was able to save him from death, and was heard in that he feared.* God heard Him because He kept saying, "Thy will be done." God hears prayers like that, aren't you glad? God heard Him because He feared. *Though he were a Son, yet learned he obedience by the things which he suffered; And being made perfect, he became the author of eternal salvation unto all them that obey him* (Heb. 6:8, 9). All that was in Jesus physically, emotionally, and nervously yearned for release from this horrifying pressure that He was under.

But the issue, as seen in this passage from Hebrews, was not whether God was able to save Him from death. God could have called twelve thousand angels who could have saved Him. But if they had saved Him, He couldn't have saved us. The Hebrew writer says, *And being made perfect, he became the author of eternal salvation unto all them that obey Him.* The issue was whether to save Him or save them. God said, "Whatever it costs, my Son, we'll save them." This salvation is for all of those who will adopt that same spirit. It is eternal salvation to all them that obey Him.

Are we totally submitted to the will of God? There are many people who are still complaining, "Lord save me. Don't let it get hard on me, Lord. Don't let me be disturbed. Don't let me go hungry, Lord. Don't let me be uncomfortable. Lord, please don't let me lose any sleep here." I want to tell you friends, if you want to save yourself, you can't save anybody else. The issue in our lives, just like His, is that if we are bent on saving ourselves and being comfortable, we will lose our power to save anybody else.

The issue for some of us is whether or not it is going to be my will or His? He was made perfect in obedience. He was made perfect through suffering. He has become the Captain of our salvation. He did not save Himself. He said, "Thy will be done."

R. A. Torrey, in one of his books about prayer, tells of a time when he was in Minneapolis directing a mission and the Lord led him to cut off all financial aid from a supporting organization and trust the Lord to supply. He did this. And day after day, almost hour by hour, the need was supplied. Torrey never expressed the need publicly; he just kept it before the Lord and God kept sending him what he needed to support his mission.

But one evening he ran out of money when there were demands that needed money. He prayed for a time that evening and went to bed, not really being sure whether the need would be supplied.

Then, in the night, he was awakened with intense pain and extreme illness. Again he prayed, "Lord, please heal my body and supply this financial need." There was no answer. He prayed again and again and there was no answer at all. This was so different from what it had been. Finally, he said, "Lord, if You see something in me that needs to be put right, that's not subject to Your will, show it to me." The Lord instantly put His finger on an issue in his life that he had known before. But before this occasion Torrey had said that the issue was too little to worry about. This time He said, "Lord, if that's really wrong, show it to me and I'll put it right."

Torrey continued, "God didn't answer, and the reason He didn't answer was because I already knew it was wrong. I prayed again, 'Lord, if this thing is wrong, show it to me and I'll put it away.' God said nothing. Not a word."

Finally he said, "Lord it is wrong and I will give it up." Instantly the pain of his body was over and the need was supplied. The finances came in when he submitted myself to what he knew to be the will of God.

FIGHTING THE STRATEGIES OF SATAN

I want to point out a second reason why prayer sometime seems futile. That is because Satan's strategy is sometimes intensified. When we pray, we are battling against the hosts of Satan. Paul said, *For we wrestle not against flesh and blood, but against principalities, against powers, against the rulers of the darkness of this world, against spiritual wickedness,* [or wicked spirits] *in high places* (Eph. 6:12). We don't wrestle with men or women; we wrestle with demonic hosts when we pray. This was true in the days of Christ. The Devil knew that Jesus was coming to be the Saviour of the world and he wanted to counteract and thwart every effort of God to bring a redeemer. That was a time of very intense Satanic ingenuity and operation.

When Jesus went out into the wilderness to be tempted of the Devil, that was the first direct encounter of Satan himself confronting a human being since Eve was tempted of Satan in the Garden of Eden. Satan knew that this was a showdown and if he didn't win it, his kingdom could be toppled. He came with desperate intensity to thwart the ministry of Jesus Christ. You know how Jesus met that? He met it with forty days of fasting. Paul said that the weapons of our warfare are . . . *mighty through God to the pulling down of strong holds* (II Cor. 10:4). Fasting is one of those mighty methods. This temptation in the wilderness was a real contest between God in human flesh and the arch enemy of God, Satan himself, and Jesus fasted.

Many commentators believe, and I would accept this, that in the days when Jesus was on earth—Jesus, God in the flesh—Satan came in the flesh with intensified frequency. There were far more demon possessed people in Judea in those days than there have ever been since. Why? Satan was counteracting. If God could send a man in the flesh, then Satan wanted his spirit in the flesh. Satan was desperately trying to block God's redemptive plan. That's why he entered into Judas. That's why he sifted Peter. That's why Jesus could say, *The prince of this world cometh, and hath nothing in me* (John 14:30). Satan was in a final onslaught to head off God's plan of redemption.

You remember that Jesus came down from the Mount of Transfiguration and there was a little lad there who was possessed of an unclean spirit, an unclean devil. The disciples tried to cast him out and they couldn't. The father brought him to Jesus and Jesus cast him out. The disciples said, "Why couldn't we do it? Why did we fail?" He said, *Howbeit this kind goeth not out but by prayer and fasting* (Matthew 17:21). When the Devil intensifies his counterattacks, then the children of God have to intensify their effort. We've got to more than match the opposition of the enemy if we're going to overcome.

An insight that I have gained through this study is that fasting is one of the special methods to intensify our efforts against the Devil. You can trace it that way in the Bible. If we cannot break the throttle grip of eating over our body, how do we ever expect to break the throttlehold that Satan has over lost men? If in our place of prayer we can't even stop eating long enough for a time of groaning and prevailing, how can we ever break the throttlehold that the Devil has over men.

I have been deliberating on why are prayers so often are ineffective today? I think the answer is that today, as then, Satan is multiplying his efforts. Why? Satan knows that Jesus is soon planning to return to this earth. He knows that He's to come and catch away a waiting bride not very long from now. You can read it in Revelation twelve. *Woe to the inhabitors of the earth and of the sea! for the devil is come down unto you, having great wrath, because he knoweth that he hath but a short time* (v. 12). We haven't yet reached that exact point, but we're getting close. I fully believe that Satan is multiplying his concentrated efforts to block our prayers, to close our eyes, to preoccupy us with secular and earthly things and keep us at all costs from the place of effective praying.

So, what do we do? Give up and quit? Go ahead and join those who want to substitute clever human programs for intense intercessory prayer? Not on your life! What are we supposed to do when it gets harder to pray? Pray harder! When it seems like God is not answering, then let's pray all the more. It didn't seem like God was answering, and Jesus prayed with more intensity, more earnestness, until sweat was like drops of blood.

Elijah praying for rain didn't stop after five efforts. He prayed until it came. He matched the demand with the intensity of his own praying.

Let me make one more point. Why does prayer some-time seem futile? Because God wants to work some changes in us while we wait for the answer. There's no other place like that of earnest prayer to see yourself like you really are in the sight of God. I have found it so in my own life.

A mighty change took place in Jesus right here in the garden of Gethsemane. He went into this garden troubled beyond words, troubled almost unto death. But an angel touched Him and lifted Him up. Have you ever noticed how calm Jesus was through the rest of His journey? He stood calmly as men with sticks and staves and torches came. He stood there so majestically, so poised, that they actually went backward and fell on the ground. Have you ever noticed how His dignity and His poise confused Pilate in the place of judgment until Pilate was under conviction? His tranquility on the cross convicted the centurion and saved the thief. His final words, just as He died, were the common words that a little Jewish child would pray just before he went to sleep at night, "Father, into thy hands I commend my spirit." He was calm. The trouble had passed.

I thank God for the change that He works in us when we get close to Him in the place of prayer. But you know, friends, the surrounding world, the pressure of business, changes our perspective so subtly and so slowly that most of the time we don't even know that our perspective is being dis-torted. We see things from such a temporal standpoint. How little you and I really see things from an eternal perspective!

Oh, the lost world around us! The lost neighbors and the lost friends who are looking on their life situation entirely from a temporal, physical, pleasureful perspective and do not see life from an eternal perspective at all. If we don't see it any more clearly than they do, how much of a help can you and I ever be to them?

God lets us wait until we see how little concern we've really shown. I do want to guard against being unkind, but when Jesus found His disciples asleep He said, *The spirit is willing, but the flesh is weak.* He knew the limitations of the flesh. But he did say that their spirit was willing. I'm afraid there are people today whose spirit isn't even willing to join this kind of a prayer battle. It's too taxing.

Paul Reece tells about a friend of his who was a minister of the gospel and went from the plains of western Canada into New York City. He was almost overwhelmed by the noise, the crush, the pressure, the speed, the movement all around him. A couple of times a week he had to go a hundred blocks or more to a hospital. He went by bus or subway during rush hour. In the crush of those subways and buses, he had to stand in the aisle and grip one of those handholds above him. The sway and the pressure of the crowd of humanity coming and going were distressing to him. Finally one day while he was there, the Lord reminded him that with his hand reached out to Heaven, why not use this as a time of prayer?

He said he began to use that as a time of prayer and the hour went swiftly. Immediately, the dread left him as he took those seasons as times of prayer. Many times, he said, he got off that trolley, or that subway, or that bus as refreshed and as calm in his spirit as if he had been cloistered away in a great cathedral alone with God. His prayer didn't change his circumstances; his prayer changed him. That's a far greater victory than if the circumstance was changed.

I would summarize by saying that if you're not getting answers to your prayers, it's an occasion to say, "Lord, am I failing of the conditions somewhere?" I can't tell you the number of times I've prayed that prayer and the Lord has put His finger on something in my life that I needed to correct. He wanted to change me. He wanted to do something in me that wouldn't have been done if there had been an immediate answer. He wants us to stand against the Devil and overcome him in this battle. He wants us to be totally submitted to His will, to bring His will to pass. He wants us to pray as intensively as the situation merits.

Lord teach us to pray.

SERMON 10

THE WORTHINESS OF CHRIST

He put away our sins! He conquers idolatry. He conquers poverty. He conquers cancer. He puts away sad and weeping hearts. He is worthy!

I'm reading this morning from the book of Revelation:

And before the throne there was a sea of glass like unto crystal: and in the midst of the throne, and round about the throne, were four beasts full of eyes before and behind. And the first beast was like a lion, and the second beast like a calf, and the third beast had a face as a man, and the fourth beast was like a flying eagle. And the four beasts had each of them six wings about him; and they were full of eyes within: and they rest not day and night, saying, Holy, holy, holy, Lord God Almighty, which was, and is, and is to come. And when those beasts give glory and honor and thanks to him that sat on the throne, who liveth for ever and ever, the four and twenty elders fall down before him that sat on the throne, and worship him that liveth for ever and ever, and cast their crowns before the throne, saying, Thou art worthy, O Lord, to receive glory and honor and power: for thou hast created all things and for thy pleasure they are and were created. (Rev. 4:6-11)

And they sung a new song, saying, Thou art worthy to take the book, and to open the seals thereof: for thou wast slain, and hast redeemed us to God by thy blood out of every kindred, and tongue, and people, and nation; and hast made us unto our God kings and priests: and we shall reign on the earth. And I beheld, and I heard the voice of many angels round about the throne, and the beasts, and the elders: and the number of them was ten thousand times ten thousand, and thousands of thousands; saying wit a loud voice, Worthy is the Lamb that was slain to receive power, and riches, and wisdom, and strength, and honor, and glory, and blessing. And every creature which is in heaven, and on the earth, and under the earth, and such as are in the sea, and all that are in them, heard I saying, Blessing, and honor, and glory and power, be unto him that sitteth upon the throne, and unto the Lamb for ever and ever. And the four beasts said, Amen. And the four and twenty elders fell down and worshipped him that liveth for ever and ever. (Rev. 5:9-14)

One reason why I know this Bible is God's Word is the way it ends. God couldn't end anything in a failure. God's Book ends in a climactic, triumphant note of victory. This book is a fitting climax to all the Bible.

John the Beloved wrote this book. I don't know how much of a problem he had finding a name for it, but I know that if some of us had had the experience John had we would think of a lot of different titles to put with it. Some of us would probably have named it "My Patmos Experience." Others might have called this book, "My Journey to Heaven and Back." Still others might have entitled it "A Hundred Million Angels." But John said simply "The Revelation of Jesus Christ." When Jesus is revealed for what He really is, He supercedes everything else. It doesn't matter what time you're talking about or what circumstance you're in when you really see Jesus.

In the portion that I have read, we see a broad vision: a vision into the past, a vision of the present, and a sweeping vision into the future. And it is all Christ-centered.

The first vision has "worthy" in it. *Thou art worthy, O Lord, to receive honor and glory and power.* The second vision has "worthy" in it. *Thou art worthy to take the book and open the seals thereof.* And the third vision has "worthy" in it. *Worthy is the Lamb that was slain to receive power.*

The first vision is of the creating Lord, a tribute for a wonderful creation. The second vision is a tribute to the crucified Lamb. The third vision is a tribute to the conquering Lion.

The Lord of the past. The Lamb of the present. The Lion of our future. And in all of it, He is worthy.

The Tribute to Creation

Thou hast created all things, and for thy pleasure, they are and were created. Who are these people who are joining to praise the Lord? John calls them the four and twenty elders, and in an unfortunate translation of our King James Version of the Bible, the four beasts. Commentators insist it should be "the living ones." The word "beast" as it is generally used in this Book of Revelation refers to earthly powers, many of whom are against the Lord. The original language here expresses the living ones.

There's some debate about who these are, and I don't propose to try to settle it this morning. The general opinion, and I think the prevailing opinion, is that the four and twenty elders express the triumphant Church. These people have crowns on their heads.

There are two kinds of crowns in the Book of Revelation. One is the crown of a king, a ruler, a monarch. That's the kind Jesus wears. Another is the crown of the victor, the overcomer in the fight. These elders wear the second kind of crown. Whoever they are, these represent the victors. That certainly would include the Church as well as the patriarchs in the Old Testament—those who have overcome in the fight and have been granted the inestimable privilege of joining before the throne. At a certain inspiration, they join together in falling off their thrones and casting their crowns before Him Who was on the throne. They begin to offer this outpouring of praise to the worthiness of our Lord.

Why are these people praising like they are? You say, "Well, they're just emotional beings and they like the emotion of the moment." This is not just emotionalism, my friends. When we praise God, some people charge us as just being caught away in an emotional spasm. I want to serve notice on you that this is far more than just a little emotional excitement. These people are very much in control of their emotions.

When the President of the United States is to be inaugurated, or appear, he doesn't come in first and wait for the crowd to gather. The crowd gathers first, and then he comes in. Likewise, the crowd is assembled here. During all of this coronation activity—with rainbows, jasper stones, sapphires, and radiant glory around the throne—these elders sit with dignity. Anybody who could sit quietly through all of that is pretty well in charge of his emotions.

But there comes a point when the four living ones begin to attribute to this One upon the throne His worthiness. We are told they give glory and honor and thanks to Him that sat on the throne. They rest not day and night, giving tribute to His holiness by saying, *Holy, holy, holy, Lord God Almighty, which was, and is, and is to come.*

I believe if any one of us could slip up before the throne today, we would hear that same proclamation going forth: "Holy, holy, holy." Isaiah heard it 750 years before Christ. John, caught up into this vision of the future, hears it going on. I judge it's been going on at every point of time in between. Why? Because His holiness is that wonderful! These beings who are closest to the throne are the most overwhelmed at the majesty and the glory of the holiness of our God. They praise Him for His almightiness: "Lord God

Almighty." They praise Him for His eternity: "Which was, and is, and is to come." They praise Him because of who He is.

But this particular outpouring of praise is because of what He has done. *Thou hast created all things.* They praise Him because He is worthy to be praised. There is no other reason necessary than that He is worthy.

The Psalmist wrote many psalms of praise. In the beginning of the Book of Psalms we have quite a few notes of melancholy. If a person had to stop with the first set of the Psalms, he would think its rather sad reading. But the Psalms do not end there. The last set of his Psalms strikes a note of praise over and over and over until they end in a triumphant crescendo of praise.

When I was a child, I was asked to memorize the 148th Psalm. I really didn't appreciate going through it verse by verse at that time, but I love it immensely today. In the 148th Psalm, David begins in the highest of heavens and comes to the lowest of earth and calls on every level of creature and creation to join in praising our Lord. And he pauses to give a reason: for He commanded and they were created. God created by the authority of His naked word.

Then He comes down to the stars and the mountain tops, the babbling brooks and the buzzing bees, and calls on men and women, boys and girls, and the creeping things and the flying fowls, to join in praising the Lord. And he gives another reason: for His name alone is excellent. Elsewhere in the Psalm he says, *I will call on the name of the Lord who is worthy to be praised.* If anybody challenges you as to why you are shouting or leaping or waving your hands, you'll just have to say, "He is worthy" and that's enough. He is worthy of all the praising, and all the worshipping, and all of the hallelujahs that we'll ever pour out before Him. He is just worthy of our praise.

The object of praise here is creation. *Thou hast created all things, and for thy pleasure they are and were created.* He created everything. These living ones, these elders, look at the whole creation from the perspective of all eternity. You and I can't do that. We look from within a little, dust-covered, cloud-laden, atmosphere-shrouded planet called Earth, and our perspective is very, very limited indeed.

I don't know if you ever get excited looking at the heavens or not. I do. There's some wonderful things to be seen there. These nights, around midnight, you can look up at about the center of the southern heavens and see the brightest constellation in all the heavens, Orion. Much is said about it in the Bible. The largest star in Orion, which is in the northwest corner, is Betelgeuse. You can look at it and probably won't even bat an eye. Betelgeuse is one of the larger stars, and if it were placed where our sun is placed, it would swallow up our sun and reach out and swallow up Mercury, and Venus, and Earth, and Mars, and reach 15,000,000 miles beyond Mars. That's a pretty sizeable star. To us it looks like a little speck. But some day we're going to see Betelgeuse for what it really is, as well as all the other stars, the other galaxies, the other constellations, and the super galaxies. We'll look upon the whole thing, and I'm positive, friends, when we see everything He made by His naked word, you'll feel more like joining them than you do right now in shouting "He is worthy."

These people are exalted and elevated to the point where they can see it all, and with overwhelming wonder they burst forth in their praise: "You created all of this." He did it with His word. When there wasn't one speck of dirt in the dirt bin, or one ray of light; when there wasn't one ounce of energy anywhere except in Himself, He spoke, and it was all done! He commanded, and it stood fast. That's why we're called to praise Him. Ye angels, ye saints, ye boys and girls, praise the name of the Lord, for He said it and it was done. He has authority in His word.

He did it, they said, for His own pleasure. That doesn't mean selfish lust; it means wise purpose. That purpose is not only past but present. That purpose is continual. These people praised the name of the Lord because they are finally enabled to see there is a purpose running through the universe.

Evolutionary scientists are trying to destroy the awareness of a divine purpose in His creation. According to evolution, that cannot be—it's all blind chance. But according to the Bible, it's all wise purpose. We can't see all of the purpose from our limited viewpoint, but from an eternal perspective you will be able to see that God's purpose is being worked out in spite of what it looks like from our limited frame of observation.

Many years ago I was holding a revival meeting in a certain place. I was kneeling at the bedside one day, and after I had prayed a while I opened my eyes and began to look at this strange, tufted chenille bedspread. I saw these little tufts of white and pink, and I looked around in amazement and thought, "What kind of a feeble mind put this thing together?" I got up and left the room thinking that whoever made this bedspread certainly didn't produce anything beautiful. But when I came back in the room and looked at the bedspread from a greater distance, there was a beautiful floral pattern spread out over that bedspread. I was so close to it when praying that I couldn't see the flower for the petal. When I backed off and got a broader perspective of things, I saw there was a wise design woven into this. It wasn't a senseless pattern of specks. It was a finished masterpiece.

That's why these people burst forth into praise. Going through this world of ours, there are times when we can't see the purpose in it all. Job couldn't detect any purpose in this suffering he was going through. You've been in places where you couldn't see any purpose in it at all. But one day, when we're raised above to a higher perspective, we're going to see that God's wise purpose ran through the whole fabric of life. What the devil was trying to spoil, God was ordering to His own glory and to the accomplishment of His own end. Well, I know enough about that this morning that I would have joined their acclamation and praised Him that His purpose is running through everything today.

We know that all things work together for good to them that love the Lord, to them who are the called according to His purpose. The devil and men and demons of Hell will never be able to destroy God's sovereign purpose. God's purpose prevails in spite of mad men, wicked nations, and tyrants.

Again, we're serving a Christ who has a purpose. God's purpose in everything is to bring many sons to glory and make them like Jesus Christ. *For whom He did foreknow, He also predestinated to be conformed to the image of His Son.* His purpose is more than to just put so many shining stars in space. His purpose is to bring together an assembly of creatures who are like Him, who are like His Son.

The Tribute to His Crucifixion

In chapter five of Revelation we see the theme of redemption that goes back into the Old Testament and repeats a practice which was initiated in the Old Testament. If a person had to sell himself or his property in order to make a living, there was a price fixed and written in a book with the hope that some day he would be able to redeem, or buy back, what had gone into slavery or been sold for his own economy. The book was sealed after the price of redemption was written in it, and it was kept that way until somebody should come along with the specified price and be able to pay it, at which time the seals were broken, the lost inheritance was restored, and redemption was accomplished.

It's this analogy that John sees enacted here in Revelation chapter 5. One great expositor of the Revelation says that chapter 5 contains the grandest event of all time, the breaking of the seals, the opening of the book. John sees the book sealed, and nobody is found worthy to open the book. Nobody is found who has sufficient funds to pay the specified redemption price and open the book. He said, *I wept much, because no man was found worthy to open and read the book, neither to look thereon.* Why did John weep? Because he grasped the significance of this momentous occasion. I told you about the wonderful creation that was made for God's pleasure. But that creation was marred, that creation was cursed by a fall. Paul says in Romans chapter 8, *For we know that the whole creation groaneth and travaileth in pain together until now. And not only they, but ourselves also, which have the first fruits of the spirit, even we ourselves groan within ourselves, waiting for the adoption, to wit, the redemption of our body.* The whole creation is groaning and travailing in pain together until now because it has been blighted by a fall, blighted by a curse. The saints of all the ages have gone down to death hoping for something they'd never seen yet. Abraham was promised a great inheritance in a land that should be his and his seed's. But he didn't see it. Isaac went to his death, and he hadn't seen it. Abraham was given a vision of a city that hath foundation, whose builder and maker is God, but he didn't see it. Isaac didn't see it. Jacob didn't see it when he died. These all died in faith not having received the promises, but having embraced them. They saw them afar off. They confessed that they were strangers and pilgrims in this earth.

In every age and every generation there have been people who hoped for more than they saw. If we hope for that we see not, then do we with patience wait for it. This has been the history of every new generation.

Is that the way the story of Christianity ends—hoping for things you never can see, following a mirage that always turns out to be vain? Well, up to this point that's the way it seems as John bursts into weeping. Is nobody going to bring the right end to this story? The book can't be opened. The redemption can't be accomplished. *One of the elders saith unto me, 'Weep not: behold, the Lion of the tribe of Judah, the Root of David, hath prevailed to open the book, and to loose the seven seals thereof. And I beheld, and, lo, in the midst of the throne and of the four beasts, and in the midst of the elders, stood a Lamb as it had been slain..* Still bearing on it the marks of crucifixion, a Lamb sits on the throne. Lambs aren't born in Heaven, lambs are born on earth. This Lamb was an earthly Lamb. This Lamb was a crucified Lamb. But this Lamb was on the throne, *having seven horns and seven eyes, which are the seven Spirits of God sent forth into all the earth. And he came and took the book out of the right hand of him that sat upon the throne. And when he had taken the book, the four beasts and four and twenty elders fell down before the Lamb, having every one of them harps, and golden vials full of odors, which are the prayers of saints. And they sung a new song, saying, Thou art worthy to take the book and to open the seals thereof: for thou wast slain, and hast redeemed us to God by thy blood out of every kindred, and tongue, and people and nation; and hast made us unto our God kings and priests: and we shall reign on the earth.* If He can't pay the price, all the people around the world who have died by the multiplied thousands under communism for Jesus' sake died in vain. Those 15,000 Koreans who were slaughtered on "Black Sunday" laid down their lives for a foolish dream if Jesus can't open this book.

But John saw the Lamb, who, with the price of His own blood, was able to break the seal. This is the story of the cross, friends. May God reveal it afresh to our hearts. We are redeemed unto God by one thing, and one thing only, the blood of our Lord Jesus Christ. He came down and identified Himself and died as one of our kind. He died in our place. He sits on the throne as one of our kind, representing us at the throne of God.

He chose deliberately to take the marks of His crucifixion with Him to His coronation. Why? Because He wants the whole universe to know that He is identified with us. That He stands for us there on the throne. He sits for you, and He sits for me. He's our champion on the throne. The crucified Lamb is in the midst of everything. The cross is the center of it all. The Lamb is in the midst of the throne. The elders, the living ones, the angels, the saints can find their way round about, but in the midst of it all is the Lamb who was slain. He is my champion today, and He's your champion there today.

I want to point out a couple of implications from this scene that are an encouragement to me. One of them is that every prayer that has ever been prayed by a saint of God, laboring under pressure, laboring under persecution, pain, privation, or poverty, every prayer they have ever prayed has been placed in a special treasure to beautify and adorn the coronation of our King. John says, *They fell before the Lamb, having every one of them harps, and golden vials full of odors, which are the prayers of the saints.*

The devil has whispered to you many times just like he's whispered to me, "Your prayer isn't going any higher than the ceiling." That's what he thinks! He doesn't know any better than that, or maybe he's lying. The fact is that every prayer a saint prays is getting through to God. God is holding it in store, and God treasures it. They're not being lost, friends. The devil may try to stop them and block them and hinder them, but God has an ear that is acute enough to hear every prayer you breathe and every desire unexpressed, and He's saying, "Just bring that here. I want to put it in my record. I want to put it in my vial." It's all going to be poured out as a fragrance up before our God to adorn and beautify and sweeten the place when our King takes His throne.

How do I know that? Well, read the story of Daniel. He prayed twenty-one days and fasted, and for twenty-one days he never got a whisper back from Heaven. He was battling the devil. He was battling the hosts of Hell. Then came an angel messenger and touched Daniel and said "Daniel, we just want you to know we heard you the first day you started praying. The devil hindered and the devil fought back, but we were hearing you all the time, Daniel." Friends, keep on praying! God is listening! Hallelujah! Our prayers are going to the throne of God. Praise the Lord!

A little bit later the incense with the prayers of the saints not only wafts up before God but is poured out upon the earth. A mighty cleansing operation takes place. Your prayers are going to get something accomplished yet folks! God doesn't answer every prayer that came out of your praying, but He's storing up your prayers, and He's going to pour them out upon the earth. Everything dirty and everything foul is going to be cleansed off the face of the earth because you kept praying. Hallelujah! Don't let the devil bluff you out of it. It pays to pray on. Just keep on praying, "Thy will be done in earth, as it is in Heaven," because it's going to be so one of these days.

Another implication here is that God is making kings and priests out of us. He's a lamb, but He's making us kings and priests unto our God. He's preparing us for a throne, and a scepter, and a crown. That's not what we were when He found us; we were filthy and vile and unlovely. But He has taken upon Himself a mighty project, to take the poorest and weakest of us who remain faithful and make kings out of us.

The kingship and the priesthood go together. Through Scripture, most of the time these functions were fulfilled by different people. There were glimpses now and then of what God wanted to do in making the priest and the king out of the same person. Melchizedek was the first example of one who was both a king and a priest.

Here in verse 9 of chapter 4 we are told that these living ones gave glory and honor to Him that sat on the throne. These are the two crowns that God gave to us in the creation. They crowned Him with glory and honor: the glory pertaining to the priesthood, and the honor pertaining to the kingship. God planned from the beginning for us all to be kings and priests. He meant for Adam to be a priest and a king. As a priest, he was to have the glory, and he was clothed with glory. He had the right to go into the immediate presence of the most high and most holy God. Adam also had the right to rule over all of nature as a king. But because he was not be faithful to his priesthood, faithful in service before the glorious one, he lost his kingship.

There are many people who want kingship without wanting the priesthood. They don't want to be submissive to the orders of the Most High. They don't want to go in and get the glory afresh upon their countenance and then go out and win the lost to Jesus Christ, but that's the business of a priest. That's the glorious ministry, and we have to have the glory before we can have the honor. We have to be faithful as priests before we can be crowned as kings.

This order is going to go on forever. In the last chapter of the Bible, we are told that His servants shall serve Him. That goes right on out into eternity. We're going to be serving Him as priests, admitted to His glorious presence and then going out to serve Him. I don't know where I'm going to be going during eternity serving Him, but I'm sure I'm not just going to be sitting under a palm tree for all eternity. God forbid! We're going to be serving Him. *His servants shall serve Him: and they shall see His face; and His name shall be in their foreheads.* And these servants shall reign forever and ever.

The Tribute to His Conquest

Finally, let's look at this tribute to His conquest. *And I beheld, and I heard the voice of many angels round about the throne, and the beasts, and the elders: and the number of them was ten thousand times ten thousand, and thousands of thousands* (v. 11). This worship celebration is getting bigger all the time. It started out with twenty-four elders and added four more, but now it's already up to 100,000,000—plus a lot more that John couldn't get around to counting.

The world's program is shriveling up. The world's program is on a collision course with ruin. The worldly hope is a fading hope. The worldly pleasure is a dying pleasure. But the saints' prospects are getting bigger from here through all eternity! Praise the Lord! We're the smallest end of the biggest thing that God ever conceived. It's growing!

Paul declared that Jesus Christ—because of His condescension, because of coming down as a man in the form of a servant and becoming obedient unto death, even the death of the cross—has been highly exalted by God and given a name that is above every name, *that at the name of Jesus every knee should bow: of things in Heaven, and things in earth, and things under the earth, and that every tongue should confess that Jesus Christ is Lord, to the glory of God the Father* (Phil. 2:10, 11). Jesus condescended to take upon Him our passion. He bore the whole of the curse. He bore our sin. Because He did it, God has exalted Him.

There is coming a day when every angel in God's vast universe—I don't know how many there are since John stopped numbering at a hundred million—will come together and join in this acclamation. Worthy, worthy, is the Lamb that was slain, to receive power and riches. And every tongue on the face of the earth, and every tongue under the earth, and every tongue in the sea—that means every tongue there is—joins in one united acclamation. He is worthy!

John calls Him here the Lion of the tribe of Judah. He has prevailed. He is the conquering Lion. John watches these scenes pass in rapid order, one after another, through the Book of Revelation. He sees all the enemies of our God assembled to come up and do their best to tear Christ out of the Heavens and take Him off of His throne. But one after the other, John sees the battles go and Christ is the Victor. He destroys death, destroys him who, by the power of death, brought people into bondage and fear all their life long.

John sees the antichrist and his armies assembled from all over the earth come rumbling together into the Valley of Esdraelon toward Jerusalem to take over the capitol of the universe. Again John waits, and the heavens open and out comes a white horse, and Him that sits thereon has a sword in His mouth and an eye that flashes like the light of the sun. As Jesus rides out on His horse, He doesn't have to shoot a gun or an anti-aircraft missile or anything else. The glory of His presence, the beauty of His face, the radiance on His presence paralyzes all of the powers of the enemy.

He doesn't move a finger toward the devil. He destroyed him utterly at the cross, and He never had to add one ounce to that. Jesus doesn't double a knuckle, He doesn't swing a fist, or shoot off a gun. He accomplished this at Calvary. It was all done from that moment on. He just tells an angel, "You get the devil and put him in this pit and get the antichrist and throw him in the lake, and let's have this done with and give the world to the saints." He put away our sins! He's going to destroy the powers of evil forever! He conquers every false system. He conquers idolatry. He conquers poverty. He conquers cancer. He puts away sad and weeping hearts. He puts away divided homes. He puts away blasted hopes. He's going to make everything right. And when He puts every other enemy away, He will place Hell in the lake of fire. He'll wipe out the stains and marks of sin. He will rule forever, and forever, and forever! No wonder John heard them singing, "Worthy, worthy, worthy art Thou to receive power and riches and strength and glory and honor and blessing."

There are two different words in the original for "power" in this passage. Verse 12 says, "Thou art worthy to receive power." This word for power means ability. The next power means dominion. What we have here is a nomination and an election. This throng of people say He is capable. He has the ability. Here's one who will fulfill His promises. Just wait until He has worked out His purpose.

Verse 13 says, "Blessing and honor and glory and power." And every voice from everywhere—the whole vast universe and every soul and every breathing thing in it—joins together and says, "I vote 'yea.' Give Him the throne. Give Him dominion. I believe He can handle it from here on out." And I believe so too.

I want us to stand and sing that song again together as we come to an end this morning.

> All hail the power of Jesus' name,
> Let angels prostrate fall.
> Bring forth the royal diadem
> And crown Him Lord of all.

If there should be any rebel in the crowd this morning and you want to come down, stack arms, surrender, and turn over lordship to Him, you can certainly do so, but we're going to stand and just adore and praise and worship Him who shall reign forever and ever.